Jen
Thanks so I
much 4 your gratefu
and care! So grateful
you were here ♡
Kruscinda

# THE VOICE OF TRUTH

# THE *Voice*
## OF *Truth*

Hearing God's Voice and Encountering
a Love that Changes Everything

# Ashley M. Edwards

XULON PRESS

Xulon Press
2301 Lucien Way #415
Maitland, FL 32751
407.339.4217
www.xulonpress.com

ISBN-13: 978-1-5456-7968-5

# Endorsements

Many Christians want to know God's will for their lives, to hear God's voice and obey his will. Yet the busyness of our lives and a culture of constant distraction make it hard--almost impossible--to listen in obedience to the guidance of the Holy Spirit. I am grateful, then, that Ashley Edwards has given us this clear, accessible guide to hearing God's voice. It teaches us about the identity of our heavenly Father, our identity as his beloved children, and practices we can engage in to hear his will for our lives. It also includes ninety days of devotionals meant to open our hearts to the leadings of the Holy Spirit. Highly recommended!

**David F. Watson, Ph.D.**
Academic Dean and Vice President for Academic Affairs
Professor of New Testament
**United Theological Seminary**

Ashley has created a book with the Father that oozes a vulnerability that is only found in a deep and genuine relationship. She shares how the Lord unlocked her heart and her five senses to better hear His still small voice. The truth in this book will bring any reader an increased understanding and revelation on how to grow in hearing the voice of their Heavenly Father.

**Jenimar Pendleton**
Founder and President
**Watermarked Ministries**

# DEDICATION

*I* dedicate this book to my indescribable Heavenly Daddy, my amazing Bridegroom-King Jesus, and my Beloved Holy Spirit—who connects my heart to His. You astound me every day with Your unconditional love. It is such an honor to hear Your voice and walk in relationship with You, my King. This book was Your idea. Thank you for coming alongside me and helping me write it every step of the way. Thank you for loving me, coaching me, choosing me, and carrying me. May this little life be a living gateway for the King of Glory to come through!

# Acknowledgements

*I* am so thankful for my wonderful family, who were so patient with me during this project. To my husband, Shawn, thank you for supporting me and encouraging me in this endeavor. You are the love of my life and I treasure you. Thank you for helping me believe in the unstoppable team God created when he joined us together… I love you!

To my four incredible children, Bryce, Collin, Madalyn, and Meredith, you are all *mighty* men and women of GOD. I am so proud of all four of you. I'm excited to see you all become the men and women God has dreamed for you to become.

To my dear friend, Jenimar Pendleton, I want to say thank you for lighting a fire under me to write this book. I am so thankful for your friendship and influence in my life. I will treasure all the many kingdom memories, but I know the best is yet to come.

I'm truly grateful to David Watson for taking the time to read my manuscript before production. I am thankful for the feedback and encouragement you have given me. It is so valuable to have help and inspiration from those who have gone before you in writing books and have experience in this area of communication.

A special thanks to Margie Johnson, who created the cover illustration, through prophetic painting. I'm so thankful for you and the time you spent on this project.

To Wendy King, I'm so thankful for the use of your quiet place at the lake that I could treasure stillness for a weekend to write. I appreciate your generous heart and cherished feedback.

Lastly, thank you to Barbara Martin, Barry Thompson, Kelly Anderson, and Tonya Duncan for diligently reading all the excerpts I sent you to review. You guys were such a huge help and encouragement to me, and I am so grateful.

# TABLE OF CONTENTS

## PART ONE: GOD WANTS TO SPEAK TO YOU

*Introduction* . . . . . . . . . . . . . . . . . . . . . . . . . . . . . . . . . . . . . . *xix*

1. Our Father's Nature . . . . . . . . . . . . . . . . . . . . . . . . . . . . . 1
2. God's Word is Foundational. . . . . . . . . . . . . . . . . . . . . . . 9
3. It Really is a Relationship, Not Religion. . . . . . . . . . . . . 13
4. Who Are You? Your Identity is Important . . . . . . . . . . . 23
5. Truth vs. Lies: Which Side are You On? . . . . . . . . . . . . . 31
6. Surrender . . . . . . . . . . . . . . . . . . . . . . . . . . . . . . . . . . . . . 39
7. The Promise of the Father: His Holy Spirit
   Dwells in You . . . . . . . . . . . . . . . . . . . . . . . . . . . . . . . . . . 45
8. God Speaks . . . . . . . . . . . . . . . . . . . . . . . . . . . . . . . . . . . . 53
9. Four Keys to Hearing God Speak . . . . . . . . . . . . . . . . . . 57
10. Different Ways You Can Hear Him . . . . . . . . . . . . . . . . . 63
11. The Power of Our Words . . . . . . . . . . . . . . . . . . . . . . . . 69
12. The Great Commission is for Everyone . . . . . . . . . . . . . 77
13. Give the Gift of Your Time . . . . . . . . . . . . . . . . . . . . . . . 93

## PART TWO: 90 DAILY DEVOTIONALS AND ACTIVATION

Day 1: I Love You . . . . . . . . . . . . . . . . . . . . . . . . . . . . . . . . 100
Day 2: You've Been Made Pure and Righteous . . . . . . . . . . 102
Day 3: Do Not Fear . . . . . . . . . . . . . . . . . . . . . . . . . . . . . . . 104
Day 4: Have Faith Beyond Your Sight. . . . . . . . . . . . . . . . . 106
Day 5: Abide . . . . . . . . . . . . . . . . . . . . . . . . . . . . . . . . . . . . 108
Day 6: Beloved . . . . . . . . . . . . . . . . . . . . . . . . . . . . . . . . . . 110
Day 7: Sacrificial Praise . . . . . . . . . . . . . . . . . . . . . . . . . . . 112
Day 8: You Represent Jesus to the World . . . . . . . . . . . . . 114
Day 9: Let Me Steady Your Heart . . . . . . . . . . . . . . . . . . . . 116
Day 10: STAND on my Promises. . . . . . . . . . . . . . . . . . . . . 118
Day 11: Connect with My Heart. . . . . . . . . . . . . . . . . . . . . . 120
Day 12: You Are My Delight. . . . . . . . . . . . . . . . . . . . . . . . . 122
Day 13: Our Intimacy First . . . . . . . . . . . . . . . . . . . . . . . . . 124

Day 14: Stand and Trust in Me. . . . . . . . . . . . . . . . . . . . . 126
Day 15: I AM Your Burden Bearer . . . . . . . . . . . . . . . . . 128
Day 16: Speak Life . . . . . . . . . . . . . . . . . . . . . . . . . . . . . . . 130
Day 17: Stand in My Love. . . . . . . . . . . . . . . . . . . . . . . . . 132
Day 18: I Will Rescue You . . . . . . . . . . . . . . . . . . . . . . . . 134
Day 19: I Gave Everything for YOU . . . . . . . . . . . . . . . 136
Day 20: I Am Your Friend and Provider. . . . . . . . . . . . . 138
Day 21: My Love Will Sustain You . . . . . . . . . . . . . . . . 140
Day 22: I Am Your Protector. . . . . . . . . . . . . . . . . . . . . . . 142
Day 23: I Draw Near to You Today . . . . . . . . . . . . . . . . 144
Day 24: Look into My Eyes. . . . . . . . . . . . . . . . . . . . . . . . 146
Day 25: I Am Your Source. . . . . . . . . . . . . . . . . . . . . . . . . 148
Day 26: I Pull You in Close to Me, Beloved . . . . . . . . . . . 150
Day 27: Intimacy Is What I Desire. . . . . . . . . . . . . . . . . . 152
Day 28: Walk in Love. . . . . . . . . . . . . . . . . . . . . . . . . . . . . 154
Day 29: I Will Fight for You . . . . . . . . . . . . . . . . . . . . . . 156
Day 30: Follow Me and Stay Close . . . . . . . . . . . . . . . . . 158
Day 31: Love Me by Following Me in Obedience . . . . . . . 160
Day 32: I Have Chosen This Generation . . . . . . . . . . . . . 162
Day 33: My Love is Steadfast . . . . . . . . . . . . . . . . . . . . . . 164
Day 34: Stay in Sync with My Heart . . . . . . . . . . . . . . . . 166
Day 35: I Rejoice over You. . . . . . . . . . . . . . . . . . . . . . . . . 168
Day 36: Fully Surrender to Me. . . . . . . . . . . . . . . . . . . . . 170
Day 37: I Am a Way Maker. . . . . . . . . . . . . . . . . . . . . . . . 172
Day 38: Come Away with Me. . . . . . . . . . . . . . . . . . . . . . . 174
Day 39: Trust Me as Little Children . . . . . . . . . . . . . . . . 176
Day 40: I Am Your Strong Support . . . . . . . . . . . . . . . . . 178
Day 41: I Am Your Anchor . . . . . . . . . . . . . . . . . . . . . . . . 180
Day 42: I AM the God of the Breakthrough! . . . . . . . . . . . 182
Day 43: My Love is Outrageous. . . . . . . . . . . . . . . . . . . . . 184
Day 44: I AM Your Bridegroom . . . . . . . . . . . . . . . . . . . . 186
Day 45: I AM your Beloved Creator . . . . . . . . . . . . . . . . 188
Day 46: My Love Defends You. . . . . . . . . . . . . . . . . . . . . . 190
Day 47: Let the Living Hope Shine through You. . . . . . . . 192
Day 48: Great is My Faithfulness. . . . . . . . . . . . . . . . . . . . 194
Day 49: I Am the One Who Heals Your Heart . . . . . . . . . . 196
Day 50: Trust Me for Deliverance . . . . . . . . . . . . . . . . . . 198
Day 51: Focus Your Mind and Heart on Me. . . . . . . . . . . . 200
Day 52: Rest in my Presence. . . . . . . . . . . . . . . . . . . . . . . 202
Day 53: My Goodness is Yours. . . . . . . . . . . . . . . . . . . . . . 204
Day 54: Arise. . . . . . . . . . . . . . . . . . . . . . . . . . . . . . . . . . . . 206
Day 55: Deny Yourself and Follow Me . . . . . . . . . . . . . . 208

Day 56: You are Partakers of My Divine Nature . . . . . . . . . 210
Day 57: Here Comes the Harvest . . . . . . . . . . . . . . . . . . . . . . 212
Day 58: Radical Love, Radical Generosity,
         Radical Mercy . . . . . . . . . . . . . . . . . . . . . . . . . . . . . . 214
Day 59: I Give You the Words of Life . . . . . . . . . . . . . . . . 216
Day 60: I AM a Good Father . . . . . . . . . . . . . . . . . . . . . . . . 218
Day 61: You Are a World Changer . . . . . . . . . . . . . . . . . . . 220
Day 62: My Love Heals You . . . . . . . . . . . . . . . . . . . . . . . . 222
Day 63: Align Yourself with My Truth . . . . . . . . . . . . . . . 224
Day 64: Rest in My Shadow . . . . . . . . . . . . . . . . . . . . . . . . 226
Day 65: Stand Up in My Waves of Mercy . . . . . . . . . . . . . 228
Day 66: The Greatest Awakening Ever . . . . . . . . . . . . . . . . 230
Day 67: Do You Trust Me? . . . . . . . . . . . . . . . . . . . . . . . . . 232
Day 68: I AM the Master Painter . . . . . . . . . . . . . . . . . . . 234
Day 69: Come Stand Near the Flame of My Spirit . . . . . . 236
Day 70: Open Your Eyes to My Plans of Wonder . . . . . . . 238
Day 71: Just Surrender to Me . . . . . . . . . . . . . . . . . . . . . . . 240
Day 72: Who Will Reach Them? . . . . . . . . . . . . . . . . . . . . . 242
Day 73: Testify of My Love . . . . . . . . . . . . . . . . . . . . . . . . . 244
Day 74: If You Don't Quit, You Win . . . . . . . . . . . . . . . . . 246
Day 75: You are a Chosen Remnant . . . . . . . . . . . . . . . . . . 248
Day 76: I Desire Wholeness for All . . . . . . . . . . . . . . . . . . 250
Day 77: The Blind Will See . . . . . . . . . . . . . . . . . . . . . . . . 252
Day 78: Let Go of Your Offense and Forgive . . . . . . . . . . 254
Day 79: Love Even When Others Curse . . . . . . . . . . . . . . . 256
Day 80: Go Deeper with Me . . . . . . . . . . . . . . . . . . . . . . . . 258
Day 81: All I Need is ALL OF YOU . . . . . . . . . . . . . . . . . . 260
Day 82: Foundational Keys of Identity . . . . . . . . . . . . . . . 262
Day 83: Take Hold of Who You Are . . . . . . . . . . . . . . . . . . 264
Day 84: Set Your Feet Upon the Rock . . . . . . . . . . . . . . . . 266
Day 85: I Am Lighting the Way Before You . . . . . . . . . . . 268
Day 86: In Me... You are Complete . . . . . . . . . . . . . . . . . . 270
Day 87: Believe Who You Are and Be Free . . . . . . . . . . . . 272
Day 88: My Unfailing Love and Grace Pour Over You . . . 274
Day 89: I Will Heal Them . . . . . . . . . . . . . . . . . . . . . . . . . . 276
Day 90: Cling to My Hand, Here We Go! . . . . . . . . . . . . . 278

Appendix A . . . . . . . . . . . . . . . . . . . . . . . . . . . . . . . . . . . . . . 281
Appendix B . . . . . . . . . . . . . . . . . . . . . . . . . . . . . . . . . . . . . . 291
Appendix C . . . . . . . . . . . . . . . . . . . . . . . . . . . . . . . . . . . . . . 293
End Notes . . . . . . . . . . . . . . . . . . . . . . . . . . . . . . . . . . . . . . . 297
Bibliography . . . . . . . . . . . . . . . . . . . . . . . . . . . . . . . . . . . . . 299

*Part One*

## GOD WANTS TO SPEAK TO YOU

# Matthew 4

Jesus answered, "It is written: 'Man shall not live on bread alone, but on every word that comes from the mouth of God.'"

Matthew 4:4 NIV

# Isaiah 55

"Is anyone thirsty? Come and drink—even if you have no money! Come, take your choice of wine or milk—it's all free! Why spend your money on food that does not give you strength? Why pay for food that does you no good? **Listen to me, and you will eat what is good. You will enjoy the finest food.**

**"Come to me with your ears wide open. Listen, and you will find life.** I will make an everlasting covenant with you. I will give you all the unfailing love I promised to David. See how I used him to display my power among the peoples. I made him a leader among the nations. You also will command nations you do not know, and peoples unknown to you will come running to obey, because I, the Lord your God, the Holy One of Israel, have made you glorious."

Seek the Lord while you can find him. Call on him now while he is near. Let the wicked change their ways and banish the very thought of doing wrong. Let them turn to the Lord that he may have mercy on them. Yes, turn to our God, for he will forgive generously.

"My thoughts are nothing like your thoughts," says the Lord. "And my ways are far beyond anything you could imagine. For just as the heavens are higher than the earth, so my ways are higher than your ways and my thoughts higher than your thoughts."

The rain and snow come down from the heavens and stay on the ground to water the earth. They cause the grain to grow, producing seed for the farmer and bread for the hungry. **It is the same with my word. I send it out, and it always produces fruit. It will accomplish all I want it to, and it will prosper everywhere I send it.** You will live in joy and peace. The mountains and hills will burst into song, and the trees of the field will clap their hands! Where once there were thorns, cypress trees will grow. Where nettles grew, myrtles will sprout up. These events will bring great honor to the Lord's name; they will be an everlasting sign of his power and love."

Isaiah 55:1-13 NLT

# INTRODUCTION

*I* was a Christian for twenty-eight years before I realized one could hear the voice of God. I had never heard anyone teach about hearing God's voice until about four years ago. A pastor I was listening to on YouTube was talking about God, how the Lord spoke to him about his life. This started me on a journey to hear God speak to ME. Once I learned how to tune into His voice of truth, listening to Him speak His love over me has radically changed my life.

In John 17:3, Jesus prays: "And this is the way to have eternal life — to *know* you, the only true God, and Jesus Christ, the one you sent to earth." In these last four years, I have begun to truly get to *KNOW* the Father, Jesus, and the Holy Spirit. *Knowing Him* is everything. On earth, we get to *know* other people by spending time with them. Not only spending time together but also having a two-way conversation. This constant intimacy is what God desires with every one of His beloved children.

With *YOU.*

He wants a close relationship with you. He wants to reveal Himself to you. He wants to speak love over you, cast away every fear that seeks to destroy you, expose the lies that keep you bound, see you walk in righteousness and purity, inspire you to be who He's created you to be, and heal every wound, especially the broken places in your heart. Even if you are unaware of them — He knows. He adores you and will speak to the desires of your heart He has placed there! He is truly more glorious than we can fathom.

He. Is. Love.

Not only does He want to do these things in your life, He wants you to walk in the truth of who He's created you to be... transforming you to be like Jesus.

> *We can all draw close to him with the veil removed from our faces. And with no veil we all become like mirrors who brightly reflect the glory of the Lord Jesus. **We are being transfigured into his very image** as we move from one brighter level of glory to another. And this glorious transfiguration comes from the Lord, who is the Spirit.*
> *2 Corinthians 3:18 TPT*

Hearing his voice about your life and then seeing things come to pass just as he said, grows your faith exponentially. In Romans 10:17, Paul says:

> *So then faith comes by hearing, and hearing by the **word** of God.*
> *Romans 10:17 NKJV*

In this verse, the "word" in the original language means [1]"rhema." *Rhema* literally means an "utterance by the living voice." So, our faith is built up through hearing God speak.

One morning, at 5:55 AM, the Lord asked me to write this book. He pointed me to an entire chapter in the Bible about His spoken Word... Isaiah 55. This scripture came alive to me as I sat there with Jesus that morning. The whole chapter illuminates our need for listening to His voice. How many want to know God's will for their life? He desires for us to know His will. He will lead us if we will surrender our hearts and listen.

Friends, we are stepping across the threshold of a new *ERA*. God is awakening His sons and daughters to the knowledge of who they are. His desire is for us to step into the destiny He's forespoken into each of our lives. We will all be a part of the greatest harvest of souls the world has ever seen. He is wooing every heart to know Him, encounter His presence, and become intimately connected with His heart.

In order to do this, we must all learn how to hear Him in the various ways He speaks. In Chapter 9, I will suggest four easy keys for hearing your Father's voice, along with ways to know that it is Him. I will also share common roadblocks that prevent us from hearing God and what to do to resolve them.

As you make time to listen and begin to believe WHO HE IS, you will find yourself in awe and wonder of His goodness and love. You will fall in love with Jesus as you hear Him tell you who you are to Him daily, and repentance and surrender will flow from an unlocked heart.

If you are alive right now, you are *chosen*. You are chosen to be a *world changer*. God is stepping onto the scene, opening the eyes of the blind, and setting the captives free. This is not only for the "lost," but also the "found." He wants us to understand the lies the enemy has deceived us into believing, lies that have kept us "stuck" in life or in bondage.

Join me on a journey to discover God's truth about your true identity as a Christian, and the divine promises God has given us defining our inheritance as His very own children. We'll examine how the words we speak have an impact and how they affect our lives. It is imperative that we believe what God says about us and speak out that truth instead of believing the lies of the enemy.

Did you know you were created to be an imitator of God? To walk in love and truth... healing the sick and setting people free from lies and demonic strongholds? As you begin to hear and obey His voice in your life, He will inspire you to step into the supernatural. As a believer, you are empowered by God because He lives in YOU.

> *Therefore be imitators of God as dear children. And walk in love, as Christ also has loved us and given Himself for us, an offering and a sacrifice to God for a sweet-smelling aroma.* Ephesians 5:1-2 NKJV

The Holy Spirit not only dwells in us, He wants to partner with us to do what He leads us toward. He is pursuing those who are lost. He empowers us to walk like Jesus walked (1 John 2:6). To do the works that Jesus did, and even greater (John 14:12). Jesus commissioned all believers to GO into all the world and make disciples of all nations... teaching them to obey all the commands He had given. When Jesus trained the disciples (and many others) in evangelism, He gave them His authority, and told them to heal the sick and tell the people that the Kingdom of God was at hand (Luke 9:1-2).

I have to be honest with you. When I began to hear the Father speak to me, I knew HE could do miracles, but I did NOT know He wanted to do a miracle *through me*. But as I listened, He began to renew my mind to the truth of His Word and His calling for us to walk in love... modeled through the life of His precious Son.

This book is broken into two parts because I believe that a well-rounded relationship with God is multi-dimensional. We need to have instruction from the Word of God, but we also need to have time where our hearts are fully focused on Him, connecting with His heart in intimate communion.

Once you have read and digested the truths of part one, I believe that the following ninety days of the devotional will be a journey of intimacy with the Father, revelation of the deep love He has for you, and a solid understanding of how He is always communicating with you. You will be fully activated as you faithfully write, daily, what the Holy Spirit speaks to you or shows you about your life and destiny in the space provided after each devotional.

The tangible love relationship that you begin to experience inside the walls of your prayer closet, He wants to extend to full-time, all-day communion with your heart.

Come experience the Voice of Truth.

# Chapter 1

## OUR FATHER'S NATURE

We were walking toward the checkout area in Walmart, when I had a thought. I verbalized it to my uncle: "Before we leave, let's ask the Father if there is anyone who needs a special touch from Him in the store today." So as we walked, we each asked the Lord that question silently. I had one sudden thought. "Fishing section". So we walked over to the fishing rods and saw a young man standing there. We went to him and asked him how he was feeling and if he needed prayer for anything in his life. He looked astounded. Andrew began to explain how he had wrapped his dirt bike around a tree two days before and dislocated his shoulder. He showed us how he could only move his arm a few inches. He also had an injured knee. We told him how much God loved him and had prompted us to find him from the other side of the store! He put down two speakers that were in his hands and said, "Man, I was going to take these and pawn them, so we could get gas and food. But not anymore."

God's love and mercy was shifting the situation. Getting his permission to pray, we laid our hands on his shoulder and prayed a simple prayer, speaking life and healing over each injury in Jesus name. The power and love of God came swiftly in that moment and touched him. Suddenly, all of his pain was gone! He began moving his shoulder in complete rotation and tears came to his eyes as he said, "You gotta be kidding me!" We began to share how Jesus had given his life to rescue him from his sin and his sickness. He admitted he was struggling with a drug addiction. He explained that he was homeless and living with his girlfriend, in her car.

About that time, his girlfriend Ashley walked toward us with a confused look on her face because she could see Andrew had been crying. We exchanged an introduction, and I told her about the Father whispering "fishing section" to me, in order to lead us to meet them. The miracle of God's pursuit of their hearts was becoming clearly evident. We all marveled at how Jesus had touched his shoulder and knee! Through her tears she added, "Well I was just sitting in the car, asking God to save us from this mess and to please help us! He heard me..." Tears filled my eyes as I knew the merciful love of God was on display. I felt the Holy Spirit prompt me to go buy a Walmart gift card for them, so they would have their needs met. We exchanged numbers and invited them to come to church with us, so we could continue to connect with them. God had reached down into the midst of a terrible situation to rescue them out of hopelessness. They realized the Father did see them, He loved them, and wanted them to run straight into His arms.

In Luke 15, we get a glimpse of the good nature and kind character of our heavenly Father. Jesus tells a parable about a son who ran away from home and blew his inheritance on wild and reckless living. Eventually, he came home hoping he could work as a hired hand since he wasn't worthy to be his Father's son anymore. But when his Father saw him coming in the distance...

> "...*Great compassion swelled up in his heart for his son who was returning home. So the father raced out to meet him. He swept him up in his arms, hugged him dearly, and kissed him over and over with tender love. "Then the son said, 'Father, I was wrong. I have sinned against you. I could never deserve to be called your son. Just let me be —* '

> "*The father interrupted and said, 'Son, you're home now!'*

> "*Turning to his servants, the father said, 'Quick, bring me the best robe, my very own robe, and I will place it on*

*his shoulders. Bring the ring, the seal of sonship, and I*
*will put it on his finger. And bring out the best shoes you*
*can find for my son. Let's prepare a great feast and cele-*
*brate. For this beloved son of mine was once dead, but now*
*he's alive again. Once he was lost, but now he is found!'*
*Luke 15:20b-24a TPT*

This is a picture of the goodness and kindness of our loving Father. His mercy picks you up out from the deep valleys, His love engulfs you, and He rescues you when you're lost—reminding you that you are His son or daughter.

## Perception

What we believe and understand about God will greatly influence how we approach a relationship with Him. For instance, if you perceive Him as sitting on His throne watching and waiting for you to mess up, so He can reprimand you and get you back in line, you are likely to feel vulnerable. Therefore, you might avoid drawing close enough to Him to hear what He has to say. On the contrary, when you perceive Him as a loving Father... perfect and holy, you realize that He gave His very life for us. He rescued you and me from the grip of sin and death, and obtained the victory for us to have eternal full communion with him—*starting now*. That perception is something totally different. With the second viewpoint, you and I will feel safe in drawing near to this Father of love.

In his book,[2] *The Knowledge of the Holy*, A.W. Tozer, a famous pastor, teacher, and author said, "What comes into our minds when we think about God is the most important thing about us." Our perception is important. Let's make sure we get our viewpoint balanced on the truth of the Word of God.

## Look at the Word

The Bible is a love story. Zoom out with me for a moment and look at the whole picture. The book of Genesis begins with God speaking creation into existence and Him walking through the garden with Adam and Eve, whom He created in

His image. His desire was for them, and us, to thrive in a beautiful relationship with Him. Then sin came in, interrupted their fellowship, and death became a reality.

Later in the narrative, God sent his Son, Jesus, to walk out the original plan of living in perfect righteousness and He kept God's original standard perfectly. He gave His life for you and me, to die AS US, so we could trade places with Him and, instead of possessing a history of sin, we are gifted with His spotless record.

> *For God made the only one who did not know sin to become sin for us, so that we who did not know righteousness might become the righteousness of God through our union with him.*                      *2 Corinthians 5:21 TPT*

Now, that is love. In the book of Revelation, the Bible concludes with a glimpse into the future of eternity. King Jesus, our Savior, marries His bride... the bride being made up of all of his true followers who love Him. We will rule and reign with Him for all eternity.

## Our Loving Father, Savior, Holy Spirit

The Bible says *God is love*. When I began to recognize his voice as "God thoughts," I was astounded by the incredible love I encountered. He will inspire you and encourage you with truth from His Word about who you are to Him. His love is unconditional. It is steady and unchanging. His love truly never fails.

> *Those who give thanks that Jesus is the Son of God live in God, and God lives in them. We have come into an intimate experience with God's love, and we trust in the love he has for us. God is love!*                      *1 John 4:15-16a TPT*

If you've ever experienced thoughts of guilt, shame, regret, or condemnation, know that those thoughts are not from the Lord. All of our negative feelings tend to make us feel as though we should run *from* God. The Holy Spirit will convict us in a way that draws us *toward* him, for repentance.

> *There is therefore now no condemnation to those who are in Christ Jesus, who do not walk according to the flesh, but according to the Spirit.*               Romans 8:1 NKJV

The Fruits of the Spirit tell us about His nature… love, joy, peace, patience, kindness, goodness, faithfulness, gentleness, and self-control (Galatians 5:22-23). He pursues our hearts with His unconditional love and unwavering truth.

The following is a loving psalm showing the nature of our Father.

> *Let all that I am praise the Lord; may I never forget the good things he does for me. He forgives all my sins and heals all my diseases. He redeems me from death and crowns me with love and tender mercies. He fills my life with good things. My youth is renewed like the eagle's! The Lord gives righteousness and justice to all who are treated unfairly. He revealed his character to Moses and his deeds to the people of Israel. The Lord is compassionate and merciful, slow to get angry and filled with unfailing love. He will not constantly accuse us, nor remain angry forever. He does not punish us for all our sins; he does not deal harshly with us, as we deserve. For his unfailing love toward those who fear him is as great as the height of the heavens above the earth. He has removed our sins as far from us as the east is from the west. The Lord is like a father to his children, tender and compassionate to those who fear him.*
> Psalms 103:2-13 NLT

There is so much in the Word about WHO GOD IS. It is impossible for me to capture the fullness of who He is in this small chapter. But I wanted to convey His loving nature toward us, His children, so that we can recognize how He speaks to us, now that we have been brought close through the blood of Christ. The truth is, He exhibits the fullness of every character trait… love, mercy, kindness, truth, holiness, JUSTICE, (the list goes on). We must understand God's nature so we can represent Him well with our lives.

## The Lord is Our Defender

Jesus is not only our Savior, friend, and future bridegroom, but also our defender. The Word of God says He is the Commander of the Heavenly Hosts (Angel Armies). Psalm 24 speaks of Jesus as the Lord of Victory, the Mighty One... THE KING OF GLORY.

> *Who, then, ascends into the presence of the Lord? And who has the privilege of entering into God's Holy Place? Those who are clean — whose works and ways are pure, whose hearts are true and sealed by the truth, those who never deceive, whose words are sure. They will receive the Lord's blessing and righteousness given by the Savior-God. They will stand before God, for they seek the pleasure of God's face, the God of Jacob. So wake up, you living gateways! Lift up your heads, you ageless doors of destiny! Welcome the King of Glory, for he is about to come through you. You ask, "Who is this Glory-King?" The Lord, armed and ready for battle, the Mighty One, invincible in every way! So wake up, you living gateways, and rejoice! Fling wide, you ageless doors of destiny! Here he comes; the King of Glory is ready to come in. You ask, "Who is this King of Glory?" He is the Lord of Victory, armed and ready for battle, the Mighty One, the invincible commander of heaven's hosts! Yes, he is the King of Glory!* Psalms 24:3-10 TPT

In this scripture, the question arises, "Who can come into God's presence?" The answer is, those who have been made righteous in God's sight. If you are a follower of Christ, then this applies to you. Then the Word says, *Wake up! You are a living gateway for Jesus to enter our world and reach people because His Spirit lives in you.* We should rejoice, that Jesus, the King of Glory, wants to come through us — as living gateways, to reach the lost.

If we are His representatives, we should be presenting HIS NATURE to our culture. God's love is amazing. He inspires us to live as Jesus did. Jesus was an amazing teacher, but He was much more than that. He was a man who walked in righteousness and purity and poured out compassion for the broken everywhere He went.

The Bible says Jesus healed all who came to him (Luke 6:19). He declared the kingdom of God was at hand and destroyed the works of the devil through healing, deliverance, and raising the dead. He sent His followers out into the city streets to do the same (Matthew 10:7,8). Being filled with the Holy Spirit and power, He modeled for all of us how to free people from sickness and oppression (Acts 10:38).

He stood for truth and justice (Matthew 21:12-13), and He even displayed how to be a servant to others by washing his disciple's filthy feet (John 13). Ultimately, He showed the Father's heart for mankind by laying His life down in humility to pay the price for every person's sin. When we say *yes* to making him our Lord, we become reconciled back to God. As we see who God is, His LOVE gets our attention. When you begin to hear His voice and the scripture He speaks, you will begin to KNOW His nature better than ever before. I believe there are no words descriptive enough to describe our wonderful, loving Abba Father.

## Conclusion

By the Word, we understand the nature of our faithful Father. He never changes. But the way in which He deals with us has changed since Jesus came to be the spotless Lamb who offered full atonement for our sins and the sins of the whole world. Because of Christ's offering and sacrifice, we were made pure and righteous in the Father's eyes. It was at this point He adopted us as his very own children. He is patient, loving, kind, joyful, merciful, gracious, and tenderly compassionate toward us as His sons and daughters. He instructs, coaches, convicts, and inspires His children. And yes, He still disciplines us. What good father wouldn't redirect his child when headed down the wrong path? We know all of this about the

Lord because the Word is our solid foundation from which we can stand. The scriptures encourage and inspire us to live in hope as sons and daughters and show us the nature of our Father's voice.

> *Whatever was written beforehand is meant to instruct us in how to live. The Scriptures impart to us encouragement and inspiration so that we can live in hope and endure all things.*                    Romans 15:4 TPT

He is our sustainer. He is our source of life and every breath. He is our EVERYTHING.

*Chapter 2*

# GOD'S WORD IS
# FOUNDATIONAL

*T*he Bible is the Word of God. It is truth. John, the beloved disciple of Jesus, records Jesus praying in the garden of Gethsemane the night before his death. He says:

> *Sanctify them by Your truth. Your word is truth.*
> *John 17:17 NKJV*

The word "sanctify" means to purify and make holy. So, the Father purifies us and renews our minds by the truth of His Word as we read it, believe it, and live it. Our God is the Voice of Truth because He speaks His Word.

In Part Two of this book, you will find many examples of the *rhema* word (spoken word) of God in daily devotions and activations. When God speaks, he draws truth from His Word and assembles it for your life and your situation. For each daily devotion, there is a listing of biblical references that I recorded from Scripture, contained in every rhema word He spoke.

When we hear the Holy Spirit speaking the Word of God in a loving tone, we can be assured that it's God speaking. The reason we need to make sure it is God? Because we also pick up thoughts from the enemy as well. He specializes in lies, fear, and condemnation. Our thoughts can come from ourselves, the Holy Spirit, or demons. (More about this in chapter 7.) The Bible warns us to take our thoughts captive to guard against the enemy's lies, as well as our own selfish ways.

> *We can demolish every deceptive fantasy that opposes God and break through every arrogant attitude that is raised up in defiance of the true knowledge of God. We capture, like prisoners of war, every thought and insist that it bow in obedience to the Anointed One.*
>
> *2 Corinthians 10:5 TPT*

The Word of God is alive, living, and powerful. The Holy Spirit can show you deeper depths of meaning even for verses you thought you fully understood. He trains us in righteousness and transforms our life to look more like Jesus, as our minds are renewed with His truth.

> *For the word of God is living and powerful, and sharper than any two-edged sword, piercing even to the division of soul and spirit, and of joints and marrow, and is a discerner of the thoughts and intents of the heart.*
>
> *Hebrews 4:12 NKJV*

> *All Scripture is given by inspiration of God, and is profitable for doctrine, for reproof, for correction, for instruction in righteousness, that the man of God may be complete, thoroughly equipped for every good work.*
>
> *2 Timothy 3:16-17 NKJV*

## True vs. Truth

It is important for us to understand the difference between TRUTH and what looks to be TRUE in our lives. The word *true* is our perspective of what is happening. The word *truth* is universal and cannot be altered. The Word of God is truth. It stands firm and never changes. God promises us that when we choose to give our life to Jesus, we are cleansed from our sin by the blood of His beloved Son. He is our Father, and we are His sons and daughters. That is unchangeable TRUTH.

We must decide to believe the Word of God (truth) over our experiences. This means choosing TRUTH over *what seems to be true*. One of the enemy's favorite tactics is to whisper lies in our ear and throw us into an emotional upheaval about our identity. One way that I find myself personally battling his lies is through comparison. I catch myself feeling inadequate and "less than" as I compare myself to others in various ways. Even my feelings can deceive me. That is why it is vital for us to know and stand on the truth.

> *Now my beloved ones, I have saved these most important truths for last: Be supernaturally infused with strength through your life-union with the Lord Jesus. Stand victorious with the force of his explosive power flowing in and through you...* **Put on truth as a belt to strengthen you to stand in triumph.** *Ephesians 6:10, 14 TPT*

"I am fearfully and wonderfully made" (Psalm 139:13-14 NKJV). "I am more than adequate, because Jesus gives me His power and strength through the Holy Spirit" (Philippians 4:13 AMP). "I am chosen by God" (1 Peter 2:9 NLT). "I am unconditionally loved" (Romans 8:38-39 TPT). "I am a masterpiece in my Father's hands" (Ephesians 2:10 NLT).

I am a voice speaking TRUTH, not an echo of the world, because I believe GOD'S TRUTH instead of what seems to be true in my life!

*Chapter 3*

# It Really is a
# Relationship,
# Not Religion

## Conversational Prayer

*M*ost of us understand friendship. There is an old saying, "If you want a friend, you gotta be a friend." In other words, you can't just talk about yourself all the time and expect to have a friendship with someone. Listening is important. Relationships are something that is shared. Both parties contribute to a two-way conversation. Even in friendship, love is involved. That is how we were created – for fellowship with the Trinity: Our Loving Father, our Bridegroom Jesus, and the Beloved Holy Spirit. Many times in Christianity, we talk to God in prayer, and then close our Bibles and go on with our day. We are telling Him about ourselves but not asking Him to share His heart with us. Many times, this is because we are unaware that He wants to speak to us. Friends, He wants us to listen. I never realized until recently, in my Christian walk, that we can talk with God in conversation all through the day. Communing with Him can take place anytime during the day or night, no matter what we are doing, because we can converse with Him in our thoughts. Many of us are familiar with Jeremiah 29:11:

*For I know the **thoughts** that I think toward you, says the Lord, thoughts of peace and not of evil, to give you a future and a hope. Then you will call upon Me and go and pray to Me, and I will listen to you. And you will seek Me and find Me, when you search for Me with all your heart. I will be found by you, says the Lord.*
*Jeremiah 29:11-14a NKJV*

And here is what He says four chapters later:

*Ask me and **I will tell you** remarkable secrets you do not know about things to come.*          *Jeremiah 33:3 NLT*

God wants to be friends with you. He wants to share his heart with you and tell you secrets. There is much love in this friendship. There is no fear because His perfect love tells our fear to run (1 John 4:18). He loves to hear your heart, as well. Our main purpose is to love God and be loved by Him.

Jesus also reminds his disciples (his friends) that His people will hear his voice.

*My own sheep will hear my voice and I know each one, and they will follow me.*          *John 10:27 TPT*

Jesus didn't come to die *just* to provide us with access to heaven. He came for us so we could develop deep intimacy and experiential knowledge of Him and the Father through the Holy Spirit.

## Don't Strive, Just Snuggle

It's so important that we understand that we are worthy to come close to Him. When we give our lives to Jesus, we are made into a brand-new person... our old person is dead. We have new life IN CHRIST (Colossians 3:9-10). We are fully forgiven. The Father sees us as pure and clean because Jesus's blood made us clean. We've been made worthy by His sacrifice.

NOTHING we can do, on our own, can get us any closer to God or become more loved or more valuable to Him. We don't have to **strive** or **work** to accomplish a checklist (such as read our Bible every day or pray for thirty minutes) for Him to talk to us. He wants to snuggle with you. To tell you of His love, just like you do with your precious children. He reminds you that you are His and He is yours. *Really.* Our increasing desire for reading more, praying, giving, and other godly behavior comes out of intimacy with God. You and I don't earn our righteousness.

> *But no one earns God's righteousness. It can only be transferred when we no longer rely on our own works but believe in the one who powerfully declares the ungodly to be righteous in his eyes. It is faith that transfers God's righteousness into your account!* Romans 4:5 TPT

Don't listen to the devil's lie that, "because of what you did yesterday," God will reject you. We can recognize condemnation from the enemy because it tends to make you feel like you should run away from God. The Holy Spirit's convictions draw you in close to Him for repentance so that you can receive His forgiveness. We must learn to recognize lies. In a later chapter, we will discuss this further.

I always say that our Father in Heaven is the BEST DAD EVER. No matter what your earthly dad was like, your Heavenly Daddy will encounter you with a love that changes everything.

## Intimacy and Full Communion

Very shortly after I began to hear the Father speak to me in my *secret place* (as it says in Matthew 6:6 NKJV), He started talking to me about something called *full communion.* He began telling me that He desired intimate closeness with His children—moment by moment. 1 Thessalonians 5:17 puts it simply:

> *Never stop praying. (NLT)*

Have you ever had a best friend that you were super close to, and with each thing that happened to you, you'd call or text them and give them a play-by-play report? Maybe you wouldn't even hesitate to tell them every detail, because you were so close, you could totally be yourself, and you knew they'd love you anyway... no matter what. BEST. FRIENDS.

Jesus showed ultimate love to you and me when He laid his life down for us – *His friends* (John 15:13). He waits on us to tell Him all the things in our heart so He can tell us who we are to Him... His bride-to-be. The depth of the relationship depends on us and how we abide in Him. Who do you talk to *first* about the happenings in your life?

Friendship with man was the Lord's idea. Intimate conversations with God began in the Garden of Eden when God walked with Adam and Eve in the cool of the day. When sin entered the picture, it separated man from communion with God and His presence. But our amazing God made a way for us. Jesus' death on the cross caused the temple veil to be torn from top to bottom – showing the removal of the separation between man and the Holy of Holies (God's presence). And that wasn't all – after Jesus' resurrection and ascension to heaven, the Holy Spirit came to earth to dwell within born-again believers. He guides us, comforts us, convicts us to walk in holiness, inspires us to live out the fruit of the Spirit, and gives us supernatural gifts to encourage the body of Christ and bring the lost to Jesus (See 1 Corinthians 12).

So now we are partners of the divine nature of God because His Spirit lives in us. Wow!

> *Everything we could ever need for life and complete devotion to God has already been deposited in us by his divine power. For all this was lavished upon us through the rich experience of knowing him who has called us by name and invited us to come to him through a glorious manifestation of his goodness. As a result of this, he has given you magnificent promises that are beyond all price, so that through the power of these tremendous promises you can experience **partnership with the divine nature**, by which you have escaped the corrupt desires that are of the world.*
> *2 Peter 1:3-4 (TPT)*

## Your Thoughts

So, because God lives in us, we can experience full communion with him moment by moment through the Holy Spirit and be empowered to live out the Word of God. In each moment of our life, we have a choice about what we choose to THINK ABOUT. Turning our thoughts and affections toward Jesus connects us to Him in communion. The Lord notices every time you think about Him or think toward Him. Hebrews 4:12-13 says the thoughts and intents of our heart are discerned by God and his Word. Being conscious of where our thoughts are going takes practice.

In the classic book, [3] *Practicing His Presence*, Brother Lawrence describes how we can learn to have a conversational relationship with God right in the midst of our daily lives. The book is a collection of notes, letters, and interviews given by Lawrence, taken from his fifty-one years of practicing full communion with his heavenly Father. The following is an excerpt from *Practicing His Presence*.

> *Let me put it to you this way: before we can love, we must know. We must know someone before we can love him. How shall we keep our "first love" for the Lord? By constantly knowing him better! Then how shall we know the Lord? We must often turn to him, think of him, behold him. Then our hearts will be found with our treasure.*

Humility is such a key factor for walking in constant fellowship with the Lord. It requires dying to self and turning your gaze toward your Father, moment by moment. This is a real picture of fully yielding to the One who gave everything for us. But full surrender is established in our hearts as we actually experience His unconditional love for us. Look at what [4]Lawrence wrote in his book about staying in the presence of Jesus in continuous conversation:

> *This King, full of mercy and goodness, very far from chastening me, embraces me with love, invites me to feast at his table, serves me with his own hands, and gives me the key*

*to his treasures. He converses with me, and takes delight in me, and treats me as if I were his favorite.*

This is so true. I think it can be said that we are ALL his favorites. His love is totally astounding and better than our earthly experience in the natural. He fills us up so we can over-flow and splash his love, goodness, mercy, kindness, and grace on others... even those who do not deserve it. In this place of abiding with Jesus, we can actually become his hands and feet.

*And as we live in God, our love grows more perfect. So, we will not be afraid on the day of judgment, but we can face him with confidence because we live like Jesus here in this world. Such love has no fear, because perfect love expels all fear. If we are afraid, it is for fear of punishment, and this shows that we have not fully experienced his perfect love. We love each other because he loved us first.*

*1 John 4:17-19 NLT*

Let me share a testimony about this. One day I walked into BI-LO (a local grocery store) to grab two items. I was walking past the pharmacy, when I saw a man and his wife standing in line. I noticed he had one elongated shoe bottom... indicating he had one leg shorter than the other. My heart started beating fast. I slowed my pace. I knew the Holy Spirit wanted me to pray for the man's leg to grow to an even length. Although I had seen lots and lots of legs "grow out," in the name of Jesus, I experienced fear. I knew the fear wasn't from the Lord. His heart was for healing for that man. I turned down the following aisle and had a conversation with the Lord. "Daddy, you want me to pray for that man, don't you?" I felt like He said, "Yes I do, Beloved." Then I said, "Lord I'm nervous. I need you to help me and make me brave." Then my next thought was, "Daughter, I am ALWAYS WITH YOU. You never go alone."

So, I pulled my bootstraps up and walked over to him and his wife and began a conversation. I usually start with asking how people are feeling. Many times, that will bring to the sur-face a need. Then I can ask to pray for them. The man agreed to allow me to pray and added that he loved Jesus. I asked him to sit in the nearby chair, sit all the way back, and extend his legs out straight. This way, I could visually see the evenness of his leg's length.

When I prayed, I just said, "Father, I thank you that you love Bill and you love to heal us. In the name of Jesus, I speak to this left leg and command it to grow." There, right before our eyes, his leg grew about three-quarters of an inch! His thick-soled shoe was not needed anymore. He told me he'd been that way his whole life. He was going to need some new shoes. Praise God, our HEALER. Because of my trust in the Lord, I was willing to step out of my comfort zone and follow Jesus into the life of one of His dear sons. As a result of intimacy with the Lord and His love, my fear had no hold on me. His love shone brightly in this man's life in the form of a miracle.

## My Journey with This *Relationship*

I was saved when I was twelve years old, having attended a Christian school through high school, and then went to a public university where I met my husband, Shawn. I always remember "loving Jesus," although I didn't begin the discipline of a daily quiet time with God until I was twenty-two. I always believed God loved me and I wanted to learn more about my faith, so I attended a lot of Bible studies through churches I was involved in.

At that time, Shawn and I had two boys, ages two and four. My third pregnancy turned out to be twins… and both my beautiful girls were diagnosed with Down Syndrome at 16 weeks of pregnancy. This news flipped my world upside down. Initially, I was angry at God with the news, feeling that I couldn't survive the situation. I struggled with trying to bury the dream of what my family would be like, in order to embrace the one I held in reality. But the hopelessness melted into day by day trust, as I stood on the promises of the Word of God. After the girls were born, my heart connected with theirs and thankfulness set in.

Although there were and still are some difficult days, His faithfulness is constant. After several years had passed, I began leading Bible studies and found myself more and more hungry to know God. I began studying about Bible prophecy and the second coming of Jesus — and eventually found myself living in fear of the future. I listened to well-meaning Christian people, who focused on what the enemy was doing, and had my eyes fixed on events going in the world instead of keeping my eyes on God. I remember sitting in my car in a parking lot, crying out for peace in place of fear. Suddenly, a verse came to mind (which was the voice of God, even though I hadn't come to recognize His voice yet). "Come to me, all of you who are weary and carry heavy burdens, and I will give you rest." (Matt. 11:28 NLT).

Peace literally flooded my car.

A short time later, I was invited to attend a short seminar about hearing God's voice. I was so intrigued. I read in John 10:27 where Jesus said, "My sheep hear My voice, and I know them, and they follow Me." Attending this seminar was really the first time I realized He wanted to speak… to ME (other than strictly through the Bible). After that, I was determined to do everything I could do to hear Him speak to me. I added extra time to my time set aside with Him. I played soft instrumental music. I got a prayer journal so when He spoke, I could write down what He'd said to me.

I came to my spot every morning believing and expecting Him to speak. It took some time before I really understood what exactly I was listening for. It was an audible voice, I'd been waiting for, I guess. But one day… I had a very clear THOUGHT. It was: "I love you with an everlasting love." And then I thought, "Did I just think that or was that you, God?" Then another thought came to me, "I am your Father, and you are my precious daughter. Just as your girls are so precious to you, so are you precious to Me." I sobbed. I wrote it down. A few more thoughts. All so loving, so accepting. I knew I had met and spoken with my heavenly Daddy.

Since that day, listening to the Lord has been one of the top priorities in my life. I wish I could say I never miss a day making time to listen, because, well I have four kids and life throws us curve balls. I'm quick to run straight back to His arms soon after though, with no condemnation (Romans 8:1). During these sweet times with the Lord, He has established me in the truth of His Word. He speaks His Word constantly. He inspires you to live it. To become it. He is so good and loves to tell us WHO WE ARE in Him. He calls you son, daughter, child, beloved, and many other endearing names. I'm constantly astounded at the way He loves. It really is unconditional.

My life began to change. The fear left, and constant peace came in its place. And deep trust established itself in me. I began to hear the Father speak to me in the car, in the store, during chores in the house, or even in the middle of moments of confrontation with others. He knows how to love us individually. He knows our love languages because He created our hearts. I began to teach people in my Bible studies what He was teaching me about, through the Word about our identity in Christ. And how to hear His voice.

I would listen to trusted pastors on YouTube teach about the person of the Holy Spirit. I love learning about the Holy Spirit. One day, I watched a video about a man praying for someone to be healed in Jesus' name and they were healed! He talked about miracles being a by-product of being a son or daughter of God, because the Holy Spirit lives within born-again believers. I was amazed! I knew that anything was possible for God, but I didn't realize He wanted to use me for miracles.

Then, as time passed, the Lord began encouraging me to step out of the safety of my boat… and pray for someone in public. Like I'd seen on the video. Now I have to tell you, my natural tendency has always been a little introverted. This was WAY out of my comfort zone. But every day, I'd listen to the Father and be inspired to love. Not only to love with kindness, generosity, and mercy; but to pray for healing for those sick and share the Father's heart of love with people everywhere. Even at Walmart.

I was experiencing Romans 12:2:

> *And do not be conformed to this world, but be* **transformed** **by the renewing of your mind***, so that you may prove what the will of God is, that which is good and acceptable and perfect. (NASB)*

My prayer constantly became, "God, I want to KNOW you."

Then one day, several years later, as we were talking, He asked me to write this book. For you. To compile truth He's shared with me, the biblical basis for hearing Him, a simple how-to, as well as my own testimony. Because, inside every testimony is the invitation from Him, for us to say, "Do it again, Lord!" He wants to draw all his sons and daughters close to Him in *intimate fellowship*. The meaning of the word *intimacy* has gotten twisted in our culture. Although it can mean sex, that is only one of six possible definitions. The other definitions are associated with closeness, familiarity, being affectionate, and having a loving, personal relationship. God wants intimate communion with you... moment by moment. He gave His life to get you back.

*Chapter 4*

# WHO ARE YOU? YOUR IDENTITY IS IMPORTANT

*W*hat defines you? Do you identify yourself through your job? Your achievements? Or what others say about you? Does your past define you?

Your perspective of yourself determines how you go through life. Life will potter and mold you if you do not realize the truth about WHO YOU ARE. *If you will listen to who God says you are, the truth will set you free.* Then, you can begin your journey toward who He's created you to be. The best possible you. Scripture has a lot to say about who you are. Although not nearly the entire list, let's look at seven important truths about your identity in Christ.

## You are a Beloved Child of God.

You are a son or a daughter of the Creator of the universe. He adores you and protects you because you are His own child. You belong. No matter what your earthly father was like, you are now fathered by the best Daddy ever.

> *And you did not receive the "spirit of religious duty," leading you back into the fear of never being good enough. But you have received the "Spirit of full acceptance," enfolding you into the family of God. And you will never feel orphaned, for as he rises up within us, our spirits join him in saying the words of tender affection, "Beloved Father!" For the Holy*

> *Spirit makes God's fatherhood real to us as he whispers into*
> *our innermost being, "You are God's beloved child!"*
> *Romans 8:15-16 TPT*

## At Salvation, You Became a *New Creation*... Dead to Sin and Alive to Righteousness.

Don't you just love *do-overs?* You get a fresh start. Well, we are told that when we are born again "in Christ," we are BRAND NEW (2 Corinthians 5:17). Our old self has died, and we are a brand-new person. This is exactly what water baptism represents. Our sin nature is cut off as we go under the water, and it is left behind. When we emerge, we are clothed in purity and righteousness. We've been forgiven and made righteous by the blood of Jesus. We've been justified and redeemed... restored back to God's original intent for us. This means we can now view ourselves as saints instead of sinners. We keep our eyes on who the Father says we are, now that we are born again, and run to Him in repentance if we sin. This changes our focus to a "son-conscious" perspective, rather than a "sin-conscious" one.

> *For in the Son all our sins are canceled, and we have the*
> *release of redemption through his very blood.... He released*
> *his supernatural peace to you through the sacrifice of his own*
> *body as the sin-payment on your behalf so that you would*
> *dwell in his presence. And now there is nothing between*
> *you and Father God, for he sees you as holy, flawless, and*
> *restored....*                   *Colossians 1:14, 22 TPT*

> *We know that our old self [our human nature without the*
> *Holy Spirit] was nailed to the cross with Him, in order that*
> *our body of sin might be done away with, so that we would*
> *no longer be slaves to sin. For the person who has died [with*
> *Christ] has been freed from [the power of] sin.*
> *Romans 6:6-7 AMP*

## You are Forgiven of Your Past, Present, and Future Sin.

Jesus paid for the sin for your whole life… and He did it before you and I were even born. He knew you and your name before the creation of the world. He gave His life to make you worthy, chosen, secure, unconditionally loved, and victorious.

> *But if we freely admit our sins when his light uncovers them, he will be faithful to forgive us every time. God is just to forgive us our sins because of Christ, and he will continue to cleanse us from all unrighteousness.*
> *1 John 1:9 TPT*

## Because of the Holy Spirit Dwelling Inside You, You are a Sharer in His Divine Nature and Seated in Heavenly Places with Jesus.

> *For His divine power has bestowed on us [absolutely] every-thing necessary for [a dynamic spiritual] life and godliness, through true and personal knowledge of Him who called us by His own glory and excellence. For by these He has bestowed on us His precious and magnificent promises [of inexpressible value], so that by them you may escape from the immoral freedom that is in the world because of disrep-utable desire and become sharers of the divine nature.*
> *2 Peter 1:3-4 AMP*

> *He raised us up with Christ, the exalted One, and we ascended with him into the glorious perfection and authority of the heavenly realm, for we are now co-seated as one with Christ!* *Ephesians 2:6 TPT*

## You Have Been Given Jesus' Authority Over the Power of the Enemy.

> *Jesus said, "Now you understand that I have imparted to you all my authority to trample over his kingdom. You will*

*trample upon every demon before you and overcome every power Satan possesses. Absolutely nothing will be able to harm you as you walk in this authority."*

*Luke 10:19 TPT*

## You are Called to *Represent* Jesus.

The Bible says we are ambassadors, or representatives, of God's love and light.

> *Therefore, be imitators of God as dear children. And walk in love, as Christ also has loved us and given Himself for us, an offering and a sacrifice to God for a sweet-smelling aroma.* Ephesians 5:1, 2 NKJV

> *Let your light so shine before men, that they may see your good works and glorify your Father in heaven.*
> *Matthew 5:16 NKJV*

> *We are ambassadors of the Anointed One who carry the message of Christ to the world, as though God were tenderly pleading with them directly through our lips. So we tenderly plead with you on Christ's behalf, "Turn back to God and be reconciled to him."* 2 Corinthians 5:20

## Jesus Calls You His Bride.

Can it really be true? Look at these two scriptures:

> *You need to know that God's passion is burning inside me for you, because, like a loving father, I have pledged your hand in marriage to Christ, your true bridegroom. I've also promised that I would present his fiancée to him as a pure virgin bride. But now I'm afraid that just as Eve was deceived by the serpent's clever lies, your thoughts may be corrupted, and you may lose your single-hearted devotion and pure love for Christ.* 2 Corinthians 11:2-3 TPT

*In the same way the church is devoted to Christ, let the wives be devoted to their husbands in everything. And to the husbands, you are to demonstrate love for your wives with the same tender devotion that Christ demonstrated to us, his bride. For he died for us, sacrificing himself to make us holy and pure, cleansing us through the showering of the pure water of the Word of God. All that he does in us is designed to make us a mature church for his pleasure, until we become a source of praise to him — glorious and radiant, beautiful and holy, without fault or flaw... Marriage is the beautiful design of the Almighty, a great and sacred mystery — meant to be a vivid example of Christ and his church.*        Ephesians 5:24-27, 32 TPT

I know for the men, this could stretch you a little, being referred to as *a bride*, but the Bible also calls men and women *sons*. According to this scripture, earthly marriage is supposed to be a clear example of Jesus and His bride, the church. Of course, just because you go to church doesn't make you a part of His bride any more than being in a garage makes you a car. To be truly saved is to be transformed into a new creation. His beloved bride will be comprised of all those who show their love by obeying the Word of God and seeking Jesus with their whole heart to "know" Him.

*Not everyone who says to Me, "Lord, Lord," will enter the kingdom of heaven, but only he who does the will of My Father who is in heaven. Many will say to Me on that day [when I judge them], "Lord, Lord, have we not prophesied in Your name, and driven out demons in Your name, and done many miracles in Your name?" And then I will declare to them publicly, "I never knew you; depart from Me [you are banished from My presence], you who act wickedly [disregarding My commands]."*
Matthew 7:21-23 AMP

## Conclusion

So... let's get this straight. God Himself comes down to earth from being eternally God (never created, always God) and agrees to step into our shoes as a man, be humbled to the point of a servant on His own accord, and to walk this thing out like it was originally supposed to be done in perfect righteousness (before the snake came into the picture). He not only came to walk a mile in our shoes (the Potter became the clay), but to love us, teach us truth, **tell us who we are to Him**, heal us, deliver us from the schemes of the enemy, and RESCUE US FROM THE GRAVE. He planned to do all this before the foundation of the world. Jesus said *yes* to the most torturous death imaginable to rescue His beautiful bride. His bride is *you*. And *me*. And every laid-down, fully-surrendered, lover of Jesus Christ. *Wow*. It chokes me up to realize how loving and merciful our God is.

Let me ask you this. Would you marry an acquaintance? Someone you had only talked to once or twice? Or would you only want to marry the one who loved you beyond a shadow of a doubt? This someone had shared their heart with you, their dreams, and even their fears. One who wasn't too shy or embarrassed or ashamed to tell others about the amazing love you shared with each other.

Being halfway committed to Jesus is just another way to tell him, through the life you live, that *what he did for you didn't really mean THAT much to you*. Actions always speak louder than words. Only "incorporating Jesus" into the edge of our life is to tell our "Knight in Shining Armor," who braved life and death to rescue us, that we're super busy and maybe we'll take hold of His hand and ride off into the sunset a little later... after we accomplish our own agenda.

The King of Glory is pursuing his bride in this season like never before. The Holy Spirit is connecting our hearts to Him in unprecedented ways. Jesus is setting our souls on fire to sustain deep love for Him.

The Song of Songs was written by King Solomon and offers a prophetic picture of Jesus and His bride-to-be. In the last chapter, I believe it speaks of these deep, consuming flames of love that this generation will experience from the heart of God. Listen to what your Bridegroom King is saying to you today. He is setting your heart on fire for Him in this season. Let the words soak into your heart from your beloved Savior:

*The Bridegroom-King speaking...*

*Who is this one? Look at her now! She arises out of her desert, clinging to her beloved. When I awakened you under the apple tree, as you were feasting upon me, I awakened your innermost being with the travail of birth as you longed for more of me. Fasten me upon your heart as a seal of fire forevermore. This living, consuming flame will seal you as my prisoner of love. My passion is stronger than the chains of death and the grave, all-consuming as the very flashes of fire from the burning heart of God. Place this fierce, unrelenting fire over your entire being. Rivers of pain and persecution will never extinguish this flame. Endless floods will be unable to quench this raging fire that burns within you. Everything will be consumed. It will stop at nothing as you yield everything to this furious fire until it won't even seem to you like a sacrifice anymore.*

*Song of Songs 8:5-7 TPT*

# Chapter 5

# TRUTH VS. LIES: WHICH SIDE ARE YOU ON?

*M*ost people know that lying is wrong. "Tell me the truth" is a phrase you've probably heard your parents say. But sometimes there's a small deviance from the truth that probably no one will even know about. We usually name those deviances *little white lies*. No matter if the lie is black or white (meaning blatant or in a gray area), all lying is sin. In the Bible, Jesus says:

> *I am the way, the **truth**, and the life.*    John 14:6a NKJV

Jesus is Truth. Adversely, the devil is referred to as the "father of lies." Jesus said to the Pharisees:

> *You are of your father the devil, and you want to do the desires of your father. He was a murderer from the beginning and does not stand in the truth because there is no truth in him. Whenever he speaks a lie, he speaks from his own nature, for he is a liar and the father of lies.*
> John 8:44 NASB

Many know they should tell the truth and not lies, but what about examining what you believe and even think? We must align ourselves with the truth and cast down any lie that comes into our thinking. This is where we must know the Word of God. The Bible is our standard for truth.

We are made in God's image and we are spiritual beings as well as physical ones. We were created to be filled with the Spirit of God and His power.

2 Corinthians 4:7 says we are like clay jars.

> *We now have this light shining in our hearts, but we our-*
> *selves are like fragile clay jars containing this great trea-*
> *sure. This makes it clear that our great power is from God,*
> *not from ourselves.*

We know a jar is an empty container. It holds material. When we give our life to Jesus, we receive the free gift of salvation, and the Holy Spirit comes to live in us. But before salvation, this jar or vessel was susceptible to the influence of spirits other than the Holy Spirit.

> *And you [He made alive when you] were [spiritually] dead*
> *and separated from Him because of your transgressions*
> *and sins, in which you once walked. You were following*
> *the ways of this world [influenced by this present age], in*
> *accordance with the prince of the power of the air (Satan),*
> *the spirit who is now at work in the disobedient [the unbe-*
> *lieving, who fight against the purposes of God].*
> *Ephesians 2:1-2 AMP*

> *Before we knew God as our Father and we became his chil-*
> *dren, we were unwitting servants to the powers that be,*
> *which are nothing compared to God.*
> *Galatians 4:8 TPT*

The spiritual realm can communicate in thoughts. "Hearing God's still, small voice" is an example. We are actually receiving His thoughts into our minds. So, it is understandable that we can have thoughts from three sources: ourselves (Prov. 23:7), the Holy Spirit (Psalm 139:17), and also the demonic realm (Luke 8:12, 1 John 5:19). With all three playing across our minds, it's so important we learn to determine what truth is and what are lies. The Bible speaks of this war in our mind in 2 Corinthians:

> *For though we walk in the flesh, we do not war after the flesh: (For the weapons of our warfare are not carnal, but mighty through God to the pulling down of strong holds;) Casting down imaginations, and every high thing that exalteth itself against the knowledge of God, and bringing into captivity every thought to the obedience of Christ...*
> *2 Corinthians 10:3-5 KJV*

We must know the truth in the Word and put on our armor. Ephesians speaks of who we are opposed to in this war in our minds:

> *Put on the full armor of God [for His precepts are like the splendid armor of a heavily-armed soldier], so that you may be able to [successfully] stand up against all the schemes and the strategies and the **deceits** of the devil. For our struggle is not against flesh and blood [contending only with physical opponents], but against the rulers, against the powers, against the world forces of this [present] darkness, against the spiritual forces of wickedness in the heavenly (supernatural) places.* *Ephesians 6:11-12 AMP*

One day I was in Target, carrying an armful of things and heading to the checkout area. I was behind a woman who was walking slowly. I noticed her cell phone had been stuck in her back pocket. It got my attention because it was about to fall out of her pocket. I suddenly had the thought, "I could grab that cell phone and take off running!" I literally started laughing out loud. I said, "Not today, Devil!!"

The funny thing was, I had just prayed for someone for healing a few minutes before. I was in a thankful mood. Think about the guilt many have because of thoughts that come through their minds and they automatically take ownership of those thoughts. We must take our thoughts captive and make them obey Christ. Each thought will reveal the nature and character of its source.

One of the most common areas in our thought lives, where we tend to believe lies, is about ourselves. Sooner or later, most people have thoughts like these: "I'm so ugly," or "I'll never achieve this goal," or "Compared to them, I'm nothing," or maybe "I am not worthy because of what I've done." Other negative thoughts might be: "Nobody cares about me," or "That promise is not for me," or "I am totally abandoned." Possibly we can think, "The world would be better off without me here screwing it up," or "I'll never be free from this addiction."

These are all lies. Funny how they all sound like your own thoughts. With hurtful thoughts like these, we can rule out the source being the Holy Spirit. Whether they are originating from a demonic source or yourself, we know these are lies. If you have fallen into the place of "if you think it, it must be your own thought," it's important to realize you may be partnering with lies from the enemy. Lies want to stay hidden in the darkness. When we recognize a lie that is contrary to what the Bible says, we need to get it into the light. How do we do this? Tell someone what you are dealing with, quickly. Once the lie has exposure to the light, you can break agreement with it and gain freedom from that bondage.

When God speaks, confusion fades. In order to know how He speaks, we study the Word. The Bible is filled with truths about what God says about you:

- It says you are created in the image of God (Gen. 1:27).
- You are beautiful to Jesus! (Song of Songs 4:7).
- You are His masterpiece (Eph. 2:10).
- Jesus lives in you through the Holy Spirit (Gal. 2:20).
- You can do all things through Christ who strengthens you (Phil. 4:13).
- You've been chosen for a special purpose and destiny (Deut. 7:6).
- Jesus made you worthy (Rev. 3:4).
- Nothing can separate you from the Love of God (Rom. 8:39).
- You are never alone because the Lord will never leave you or forsake you (Deut. 31:6).
- When you believe the truth, the truth will set you free (John 8:32).

Having agreement in a situation is powerful. The Bible is clear that agreement is important. We should be aligning our belief system with that of the Word of God.

*Again, truly I tell you, if two of you agree on earth about anything you ask, it will be done for you by my Father in heaven.*                                           *Matthew 18:19 NIV*

In the same way as prayer, we can come into agreement with the truth we believe. It's one thing to read in the Bible that you're a child of God, but it's another thing to actually *believe* it about yourself and therefore act like it. God wants us to not only read the Word, but to do what it says or, in other words, partner with the truth.

When we come under the influence of a lie in our thinking or belief, we are held captive by it. As we believe the liar (Satan), we come under his influence.

*Don't you realize that you become the slave of whatever you choose to obey? You can be a slave to sin, which leads to death, or you can choose to obey God, which leads to righteous living.*                                         *Romans 6:16 NLT*

*Gently instruct those who oppose the truth. Perhaps God will change those people's hearts, and they will learn the truth. Then they will come to their senses and escape from the devil's trap. For they have been held captive by him to do whatever he wants.*                    *2 Timothy 2:25-26 NLT*

But there is HOPE. The moment we break agreement with the lie and, instead, partner with the truth of the Word, miracles are released, and prison doors are opened.

I was a part of a prayer ministry at a church I attended. One day, a gentleman came hobbling in for prayer. He had extreme pain in his knee. We began to pray for his knee to be healed. After several prayers, his knee pain remained the same. So we began to talk with him about his life and found out that he had battled addiction to prescription pain medications. He had tried to quit many times, but always seem to fall back into it. He expressed a desire to be free. So we led him in a prayer to *repent* from overusing the drugs (repent just means to change your mind and go the opposite way), then to break agreement with addiction and the lie that he would never be free (that he had believed). When we finished the prayer, he jumped up, and, without any further prayer for healing, his knee was totally healed. He decided to partner with the truth that repentance and the blood of Jesus brings freedom and victory over every addiction and sickness. He came into agreement with the truth and then he experienced glorious freedom from addiction and pain.

## Deliverance from the Spirit of Fear.

I wanted to share a testimony about how the Shepherd of our soul, JESUS, is in pursuit of our hearts. He desires to open the eyes of the blind and set the captives free. It says in Isaiah 42:7:

> *You will open the eyes of the blind. You will free the captives from prison, releasing those who sit in dark dungeons... (NLT)*

When I first read this scripture, I thought it was referring to healing. But the more I studied, the more I understood it to mean opening people's eyes to God's truth and setting the captives free from lies and strongholds of the enemy.

One morning, I was sitting with the Lord, listening, and He directed me to Psalm 91. In the first verse, it says, "He who dwells in the secret place of the Most High shall abide under the shadow of the Almighty."

I began hearing the Father tell me that his shadow was not dark like earthly shadows but is illuminated with peace beyond understanding, because it's a space close to Him. He said He was pursuing those who were wandering from truth... those who are called by His name, who will move in sync with His heart to shift things on earth. He said, with His pursuit, enemies flee! Demons shudder in His presence, and they hide when His light shines.

They come back to lie and deceive us, to try and convince us that deliverance and healing didn't really happen. But as His revelation light shines toward them and their lies, they will run. The only power they have is to deceive you into believing them instead of the truth. The Lord continued, "Cling to Jesus! The way, the truth, and the life. Where truth reigns, there is freedom. And where freedom is, there is peace… the Prince of Peace."

With a thankful heart, my day cranked up with getting my children to school and grabbing breakfast for a friend and me. I was taking her food because she was recovering from surgery. We ate and talked and eventually got into a conversation about her dealing with fear. She had unprecedented fears about many things, like dying. This fear plagued her, even though she was young and in the picture of health. She was even struggling with both being alone and going in public because of fear. My heart swelled with compassion for her. It was like she was being held captive by the enemy's lies comprised of fearful thoughts.

I asked if I could pray for her. With her agreement, I began to pray for her, and the words the Father had spoken to me that morning came to mind and flowed from my mouth. Then I began to thank Jesus for his RADIANT LOVE which casts out every fear. I turned to her and looked into her tear-filled eyes and asked her to repeat some phrases in order to come out of agreement with the lies she had been believing. She spoke phrases such as, "I break agreement with the lie that I'm going to die. I break agreement with fear in every way! I am in my Father's hands. His extreme love for me casts out every one of these fears!"

The love of Jesus and the Holy Spirit's presence just poured over her, and all we could do was cry tears of joy. As we sat there processing the Lord's pursuit of her heart, we realized the words He'd said to me that morning were meant for her. She recounted that, as I'd prayed, God gave her a vision of her, hiding in the dark shadows, captive to fear… but when the words were spoken about God shining his revelation light on the darkness and the demonic fleeing, she began to see herself in a field of beautiful flowers with light all around. The fear was gone, and, in its place, she had freedom.

As she spoke out her agreement with God's truth instead of those nasty lies, her freedom was made manifest. It was such a beautiful moment that brought my friend healing, freedom, and a connection with the heart of her Bridegroom-King. Since that day, she has been free of the plaguing fear because she's learned how to take her thoughts captive when fear or lies try to gain entrance. Send those thoughts to the feet of Jesus. Praise our incredible Father, whose promises are a firm foundation to stand.

Testimonies are amazing because as we share them, it's an invitation to BELIEVE God wants to do it again. Again... for you.

Are there any lies you believe? Is there an area of your life in which you feel stuck, imprisoned, or hopeless? Begin filling your mind with what the Bible says about your situation. Write them down. (For scriptures about your identity in Christ, see Appendix A.) Feelings may seem loud in your life, but they aren't always true. Come out of agreement with what the demonic realm wants you to believe and into agreement with the Word of God and what the Holy Spirit whispers across your mind and heart. You, too, can be set free.

> *And you shall know the truth, and the truth shall make you free.*                                     *John 8:32 NKJV*

*Chapter 6*

# SURRENDER

---

*In* our Western culture, much of our talking begins with the word "I." I'm guilty, too. We tend to have *me-first* thinking. Many are consumed with themselves, and they are number one in their own world. Apple Computers have picked up on this and have named many of their products using this same concept. Among them are the: iPhone, iFit, iPad, iPod, and iLife.

## But It's Not About You

Although selfishness is part of the sinful nature we are all born with, at salvation, we become a brand-new creation. Many have not fully understood what salvation actually means. In the past, there has been a focus on praying a specific prayer and receiving a ticket to heaven. Then, people go along with their lives as normal, thinking if they make it to church on Sunday, they're just fine with God.

But, being a Christian changes everything, because it is about transformation. Other sincere Christians want to live for God, but don't want to let go of sin habits or can't seem to kick them. Certain things in their lives continually distract and pull them away from having the time to spend with Jesus.

I heard Todd White, a teacher and equipper of our identity in Christ as children of God, term this half-way committed style of Christianity as "Jesus incorporated". Instead of being ALL IN, you incorporate Jesus into your life without being willing to give him ALL OF YOU. It's like putting your big toe in the water instead of JUMPING IN. Or you ask Him to come into your house but tell him he needs to stay in the foyer and living room. You aren't ready for Him to see all the rooms... much less give Him full control. But this is not what the Bible asks of us. Jesus wants our full surrender.

> *Then Jesus said to his disciples, "If you truly want to follow me, you should at once completely reject and disown your own life. And you must be willing to share my cross and experience it as your own, as you continually surrender to my ways. For if you choose self-sacrifice and lose your lives for my glory, you will continually discover true life. But if you choose to keep your lives for yourselves, you will forfeit what you try to keep. For even if you were to gain all the wealth and power of this world with everything it could offer you – at the cost of your own life – what good would that be? And what could be more valuable to you than your own soul?"*                    *Matthew 16:24-26 TPT*

If we want to be followers of Jesus, we must die to ourselves. To lay down our own way. This is called SURRENDER. Until we decide to give God our whole heart and whole life, we will not experience all He has for us. He wants you to open every room of your heart to Him so he can lavish you with love and healing. Pride is an enemy to full and complete surrender. We must lay down pride and become humble. Humility is not thinking less of yourself (self-condemnation), it's thinking of yourself LESS. It's going low to serve others in strength. Don't be afraid of transparency before Him: He knows it all, anyway. Being transparent, or vulnerable, is an attitude of the heart in which you show your trust of the other person.

Maybe you're wondering how someone can do this *surrender thing*. A desire to fully surrender to the Lord comes naturally when we begin to KNOW Him and experience His love casting out our fear. The Bible says eternal life in Christ begins as soon as we give our life to Jesus and we then become "born again" (see John 3:1-21).

Jesus said, in John 17:3, that eternal life was to *know* the Father and the Son. *Know* in the original language goes beyond just intellectual knowledge and understanding. It means to encounter or experience an intimately close, ongoing relationship. Intimate relationships are usually characterized spending a lot of time together and by sharing conversations about personal, innermost thoughts. Devotion and enduring love are developed here. Did you know Jesus laid His life down to establish a beautiful love relationship with you? Being a Christian is about having this type of close relationship with the Father, the Son, and the Holy Spirit. And it begins when we listen to His voice and connect with His heart.

Jesus modeled full surrender with his life. As a member of the Trinity (Father, Son, and Holy Spirit), our eternal God became human. He laid aside His divine nature temporarily to become one of us. Being without sin, He fulfilled the requirement of God's law perfectly, in order to become the spotless Lamb of God. He submitted fully to His Father's will to die on the cross in order to take the sins of the whole world on His shoulders. He gave everything for you.

> *You must have the same attitude that Christ Jesus had. Though he was God, he did not think of equality with God as something to cling to. Instead, he **gave up his divine privileges**; he took the humble position of a slave and was born as a human being. When he appeared in human form, he humbled himself in obedience to God and died a criminal's death on a cross.* Philippians 2:5-8 NLT

Jesus fully surrendered to the Father in becoming a man, and then every day during His life here on earth He maintained this yielding. He was so surrendered to the Father, Jesus said that He could do nothing of himself.

> *Then Jesus answered and said to them, "Most assuredly, I say to you, the Son can do nothing of Himself, but what He sees the Father do; for whatever He does, the Son also does in like manner."* John 5:19 NKJV

> *Don't you believe that the Father is living in me and that I am living in the Father? Even my words are not my own*

*but come from my Father, for he lives in me and performs his miracles of power through me.*      John 14:10 TPT

He modeled this full surrender so we would know how to do it, just like He did.

In life, we constantly have choices. Surrendering to the plan of God for our lives involves including the Lord on choices you have every day. This includes where you go for lunch or even what you do with spare time. For instance, yesterday I had a doctor's appointment at 9:15 AM, but I was set to arrive about forty-five minutes early. I was planning to sit in my car and work on this chapter about surrendering to Jesus. But on my drive there, I had a picture in my mind of me sitting on the benches outside the front entrance of the hospital, located across the street from my doctor's office.

I asked the Lord, "Daddy, do you want me to do that with my extra time instead? To go sit on the bench and look for people to encourage, love on, and pray for?" My next thought was, "Yes, Beloved, trust me." So I had a choice. Was I making it up? Was I going to risk it? It sure would be EASIER to sit in my car and work on this chapter. But then I realized He knows all things. His ways are higher and better! He is trustworthy. He is good. If I'm operating in a life of surrender, it will look like *something*.

I decided to go. I immediately saw a sweet lady sitting outside, and we struck up a conversation as soon as I sat down with her. Her grandson had been shot and paralyzed as a result of making bad choices. He was only seventeen. She looked so weary. I got to love, encourage, and pray for her and her grandson. She was a believer and had been praying for his salvation. I got to share with her the reason I was there that day, that Jesus had heard her prayers and wanted to tangibly love on her with another one of His own. She thanked me through her tears, and I hugged her and left.

*Wow.* If we could only be willing to surrender and become His hands and feet. He is so good, and he wants to shine His love and goodness into this world through you.

# A Prayer of Surrender

Heavenly Father, I completely surrender all my life to You. I adore You, for You are mighty and all-powerful, worthy of all my praise. Today, I call on the beautiful name of my Lord and Savior, Jesus Christ to forgive me from withholding parts of my life and heart from You. I completely surrender my will to Yours. Unlock every door of my heart and heal me. I thank You for the gift of life and for filling me with purpose. Fill me with Your Holy Spirit and lead me in every decision I make. I want to hear Your voice in every situation. I thank You for the opportunities You will give me to live for You and to walk in complete obedience. Thank you, Lord. I love You with all my heart and soul and mind. In Jesus' mighty name, Amen.

*Chapter 7*

# THE PROMISE OF THE FATHER: HIS HOLY SPIRIT DWELLS IN YOU

## Who is HE?

*B*efore Jesus died on the cross, He told His disciples that even though He couldn't stay with them, an even more complete source of constant help was being given to each of them. It was a gift from God. Actually, the gift WAS God… the Holy Spirit of God.

> *And I will pray the Father, and He will give you another Helper, that He may abide with you forever – the **Spirit of truth**, whom the world cannot receive, because it neither sees Him nor knows Him; but you know Him, for He dwells with you and will be in you.* John 14:16-17 NKJV

The Holy Spirit is one of the three members of our eternal God we term the *Trinity*. He is not a force or just simply a power. He is a person. He loves us just as the Father and Jesus do. Isn't it astounding when you think about the provision of our amazing God? He came and paid the price for us to be made right with Him through the life of Jesus, then sent the person of the Holy Spirit to live in us to EMPOWER us to live out what the Bible calls us to. If He is willing to do these things for us won't He also give us all things? He's so worthy of all our praise, forever.

Holy Spirit is called the Spirit of Truth. He reveals the truth to us from the Word of God (Logos) and from the heart of God... His spoken word (Rhema).

> *When the Spirit of truth comes, he will guide you into all truth. He will not speak on his own but will tell you what he has heard. He will tell you about the future.*
> *John 16:13 NLT*

He will not only help us understand the words we read in the Bible, but He will also speak about what God has planned for our lives and the lives of our loved ones.

Usually someone's last words are pretty important. Well, Jesus' last words were about a very special promise from the Father. He was going to pour out His Spirit upon all flesh.

> *Listen carefully: I am sending the Promise of My Father [the Holy Spirit] upon you; but you are to remain in the city [of Jerusalem] until you are clothed (fully equipped) with power from on high.*
> *Luke 24:49*

Most of us know about this event in the life of the early church. Even though it happened about 2000 years ago, we are still in the last days. But we are closer than we have ever been to the return of our Savior. And this verse is being played out among us before our very eyes. The Holy Spirit is chasing after many lost sons and daughters to come to the heart of the Father through the finished work of Jesus.

He seems to be committed to restoring believers' hearts to our "first love"... Jesus Christ. He is also establishing our confidence in our identity in Christ and wooing us to live in intimacy and full communion with our Father. This manifests in our lives as *lovers who work* rather than *workers who love.* Our desire to do the work of the kingdom grows out of our love and devotion to Jesus. We don't have to work to be loved because we've been made right in God's eyes (2 Corinthians 5:21). We are created to live in union with God. This is through the Holy

Spirit who dwells in us. The Bible says that our spirit is one with the Holy Spirit.

> **But the person who is joined to the Lord is one spirit with him**. *Run from sexual sin! No other sin so clearly affects the body as this one does. For sexual immorality is a sin against your own body. Don't you realize that your body is the temple of the Holy Spirit, who lives in you and was given to you by God? You do not belong to yourself…*
> 1 Corinthians 6:17-19 NLT

He connects our hearts and our thoughts with heaven. It's through the Holy Spirit living in us that Jesus also lives in us. Romans 8:9 refers to the Spirit the "Spirit of Christ." And in 1 Corinthians 2:16 it says:

> *For, "Who can know the Lord's thoughts? Who knows enough to teach him?" But we understand these things, for we have the mind of Christ.*
> 1 Corinthians 2:16 NLT

## Coming into His Presence to Listen

God's presence is with us always, everywhere we go. King David said there was nowhere that he could escape God's presence. This is called God's *omnipresence*. It means He is everywhere present, even if we can't tell He is there. But there are times when He manifests His presence to us. *Manifest* means to display or show by one's acts or appearance; demonstrate. When the Lord manifests His glory and presence to us, it is a tangible experience.

We need to create a space and time where we can come into His manifest presence. In Matthew 6, Jesus talked about going into your own secret place to pray and be alone with God.

> *But you, when you pray, go into your room, and when you have shut your door, pray to your Father who is in the secret place; and your Father who sees in secret will reward you openly.* Matthew 6:6 NKJV

Having time alone with God is not an added bonus; it is a necessity. Making time to be with Jesus is literally the most important moments of our entire day. This is where we seek Him, and come into His presence through worship, reading, talking to Him, and most importantly, listening to His heart. It is a time that we get filled up with living water from Jesus (John 7:38) and receive encouragement, refreshment, and inspiration to walk in love and in our true identity.

Truly though, the most paramount purpose of this sweet time with God is just *being with him* in His incredible presence... not to get something from Him, but desperately desiring to know his heart and his ways. He loves to meet us in that place of humility.

Naturally then, the "secret place" is a target of the enemy. We must be very intentional in planning and setting aside time with God. I will even go to the extreme of saying it needs to be FIERCELY GUARDED, so that distractions don't interfere!

## His Presence is the Center

In the Bible, Israel would make their camp around the *tabernacle* that God instructed Moses to build. This was the place where God's presence would dwell. The presence of God was always postured in the center of the people. Today, though very well-meaning, we center our time at church on Sunday around a sermon. Many times, churches have such a specific schedule to adhere to, it gives the Holy Spirit very little room to move and have His way. Although when He is given space to lead, everything changes as we encounter His incredible presence and love.

When we meet with our Father alone daily, we have an opportunity to posture or position ourselves, to come into His wonderful presence. In humility and awareness of His unequaled majesty, we can come before him expectant of His desire to connect with our hearts. In His manifest presence, we are deeply impacted in every way.

I've always been amazed by the paradox of how we can walk with God as His son or daughter BOTH in the Fear of the Lord (absolute awestruck wonder and holy fear) and also be swept away in intimate closeness as He brings us in close to His heart. The Eternal God of the Universe, who breathed everything into existence, knows your name and chose you to live in such a time as this. He rescued you, lives in you to empower you to advance His kingdom. He pulls you in close to experience a love like you've never experienced before.

## How Can We Come into His Manifest Presence?

Let's look at a few things we can do to position our hearts toward Him. In Hebrews, it speaks of the temple veil being torn from top to bottom in the Holy of Holies, which symbolizes the separation being removed between His holy presence and man. This veil was sixty-feet tall and four-inches thick. When it was torn from top to bottom, right after Jesus gave up his last breath, this indicates a supernatural tearing. Yes, Jesus' death purchased so much more than a "heaven ticket," it brought restoration between God's presence and man... and restored us back to God's plan before we fell into sin in the garden.

> *And so, dear brothers and sisters, we can boldly enter heaven's Most Holy Place because of the blood of Jesus. By his death, Jesus opened a new and life-giving way through the curtain into the Most Holy Place. And since we have a great High Priest who rules over God's house, let us go right into the presence of God with sincere hearts fully trusting him. For our guilty consciences have been sprinkled with Christ's blood to make us clean, and our bodies have been washed with pure water.*
> *Hebrews 10:19-22 NLT*

Let's tune our hearts in to becoming aware of his presence and hearing His voice with a few keys from this scripture.

1. Acknowledge the Holy Spirit is there with you and invite Him to come close to you.
2. With a sincere and childlike heart, trust that He will meet you there.

3. Confess any sin and offer repentance and thanksgiving for the forgiveness He gives through Christ's blood, which was shed on the cross.
4. Focus the eyes of your heart on God as you praise Him and WORSHIP. Worship is such an important part of experiencing His tangible presence.
5. Wait, pray, and LISTEN.

## My First Experience with His Manifest Presence

In October 2016, I attended a Power and Love Conference with a ministry called *Lifestyle Christianity*. On Friday night, Robby Dawkins gave a message and, afterward, he said he was going to invite the Holy Spirit's presence to come and encounter us. He said when He came, we may feel His tangible presence as tingling, heat, weight on our body, extreme peace, goosebumps, or other sensations. He said some would feel like laughing, others may cry. I was so excited! I had attended conservative-style churches all my life and had never experienced the Lord like this. He invited the Holy Spirit into the room, and we postured ourselves to receive whatever He wanted to give us. We were standing quietly, but expectant, with our hands out—palms up like we were waiting to receive a gift. There were probably seven-hundred-plus people in the room.

After a period of minutes, I started to feel a tingling go through my whole body. PEACE. No fear. It was like the love of God washed over me. My hands dropped slowly down until they touched my thighs because they were so heavy. His presence was beautifully weighty. I began crying. Other people started crying and some laughed. I dropped to my knees and felt the intense need to confess sin before His mighty presence. Then, suddenly, I had this sound began to bubble up from within me. I started praying in the Spirit for the first time. What an amazing experience. I just remember that I wanted to stay there forever. It was an unforgettable experience with the beloved Holy Spirit.

## Your Turn!

Make yourself a DAILY appointment to meet with the Father, the Son, and the Holy Spirit. Prepare the attitude of your heart, confess your sin, and fix your eyes on His beauty as you worship. Read His Word and give him your attention so He can speak to you. Come expectantly and wait patiently. You will experience Him and His incredible love. When you seek Him with all your heart, you *will* find Him! (Jeremiah 29:13) Let's become faithful to meet with him daily to experientially know Him and His love. It will change your life.

*Chapter 8*

# GOD SPEAKS

## He Speaks to His Children

*O*ne of the most amazing privileges of being a son or a daughter of the Most High God is that we become equipped at Salvation with the Holy Spirit and can hear God's voice. Hearing God is not a gift. It is a birthright.

> Jesus said, "**My own sheep will hear my voice** and I know each one, and they will follow me."
>
> *John 10:2 TPT*

He expects us to listen to Him. The verse's meaning might elude us just a little because we are not that familiar with the ways of shepherds with their sheep as they were in Jesus' day. The sheep were completely dependent on their shepherd. They trusted him with their life. They knew his voice so well. They knew his ways. It's so important that we make time to listen to OUR SHEPHERD. We live in a fast-paced era of constant noise and intense distractions. We have to experience quiet spaces with intentionality.

## He Speaks in Different Ways

There are so many ways God communicates with us. He so creative. If you are a believer, you've already experienced some of His methods, even if you weren't aware it was the

Lord. I think some think they are listening for an audible voice. Although God does speak this way, it's definitely less common. His Spirit communicates with us through His WORD, through nature, music, other people's words, thoughts and mental impressions (like a quick picture or memory in your mind), emotions and feelings, our five senses, trances, dreams, visions, angelic visitations, and even visitations from Jesus Himself. I have also experienced Him speaking and leading me through themes that are confirmed over and over. For instance, for several weeks straight, I would see the number 333. On the clock, on my phone, billboards, a verse of the day, exact change of $3.33, etc. The Lord had been talking me in my quiet time about *"telling me secrets"* as it speaks of in Jeremiah:

> *Ask me and I will tell you remarkable secrets you do not know about things to come.* Jeremiah 33:3 NLT

## Still Small Thoughts

Although it can be said that our Creative God can speak to each of us differently, we can all pick up the still, small thoughts that are extremely "light" — like a feather. Sometimes they come and go so quickly we could easily miss them. This is one reason why the Lord asks us to be still before him. Not only to honor Him with the gift of time but to silence the many distractions vying for our attention. This quiet place is where we practice hearing these still, small thoughts. Then, as we become more and more familiar with his voice, we will "hear" him wherever we are.

> *Be still and know that I am God. I will be exalted among the nations; I will be exalted in the earth!*
> Psalm 46:10 ESV

The prophet Elijah also heard the still, small voice of God. God is able to speak any way he chooses, but many times it's through his spontaneous thoughts to your mind and heart.

*Then He said, "Go out, and stand on the mountain before the Lord." And behold, the Lord passed by, and a great and strong wind tore into the mountains and broke the rocks in pieces before the Lord, but the Lord was not in the wind; and after the wind an earthquake, but the Lord was not in the earthquake; and after the earthquake a fire, but the Lord was not in the fire; and after the fire **a still small voice**.*
*1 Kings 19:11-12 NKJV*

This is a common way that the Lord speaks to us, and the enemy works overtime planting doubt in our hearts that it's not really God connecting with us. Maybe you've tried hearing Him but came to the conclusion in your thinking that it's "Just your own thoughts," or, "I must've just made that up," or even the accusation—"How dare you say one of your own thoughts be GOD!" The way to combat this opposition is to keep going. Press on. Continue listening. Don't come into agreement with the lies, but believe the Bible when Jesus says, "My sheep will hear my voice." Believe God, and tell the enemy, NOT TODAY. If you don't quit, you will hear Him and experience a love that changes everything.

*Chapter 9*

# FOUR KEYS TO HEARING GOD SPEAK

## Do You Believe?

*W*e've all been there. You know, that place where you've tried something and failed a couple of times. There's something about failure that continues to whisper lies in your mind, like: "You can't," "You might as well not try," "Things never work for you," "You're just going to fail again!" or "You'll NEVER be able to hear God!" This is where you have to decide whether you are going to believe God or the devil. The Bible says,

> *My sheep hear My voice, and I know them, and they follow Me.*                              *John 10:27 NKJV*

Jesus is the Shepherd and **you are a sheep — if you have given your life to Him**. Have you given your life to Him? (If you're not sure… stop right here. If you've never given your life to Jesus, but you want to, turn to Appendix B right now. Take care of it right now! He is calling your name. If you are positive you are one of His "sheep," just believe that you CAN hear him.

JUST BELIEVE.

When we recognize we are believing a lie instead of the truth, we have to break agreement with that lie. As we saw before in Chapter 6, when we come under the influence of a lie in our thinking or belief, we are held captive by it. As we believe the liar (Satan), we come under his influence. There is power in speaking words out loud (more on this in Chapter 12). So in prayer, repent and break agreement with the lie saying that you CAN'T hear your Shepherd and declare the truth of the Word of God. Align yourself with truth.

> *Dear Heavenly Father, I know that You always hear me. Thank you for loving me, saving me, and pursuing my heart. Please forgive me for believing the lie that I can't hear Your voice as the Shepherd of my soul. I break agreement with that lie right now, in Jesus' name. I declare that I can hear Your voice because I am a child of God and Your beloved Holy Spirit lives in me. I come, expectant, to Your throne room today to hear You speak life into me. I love You, Lord. In Jesus' name, Amen.*

Our wonderful Savior is so faithful to draw near to us when we draw near to Him.

> *So then, surrender to God. Stand up to the devil and resist him and he will turn and run away from you. Move your heart closer and closer to God, and he will come even closer to you...*        *James 4:7-8 TPT*

## Four Easy Keys to Hearing God Speak

Jesus said we needed to come to Him *with faith, like a child*. Sometimes, we as adults "think too much" and sometimes we think "we have it all figured out." I heard someone say once, "The only sure barrier to gaining truth is to assume you already have it!" Let's instead come to God with a heart to hear Him speak to us, coming with teachable spirits and willingness to receive what He has for us, as a loving Father.

> *Jesus called a little one to his side and said to them, "Learn this well: Unless you dramatically change your way of thinking and become teachable, and learn about heaven's*

*kingdom realm with the wide-eyed wonder of a child, you
will never be able to enter in."*          *Matthew 18:2-3 TPT*

The FIRST KEY is to **get alone, be quiet, and be still**. This
may be a challenge for us in an extremely faced-paced age,
but it can be done. Choose a time during the day when there
are fewer distractions. I love the early mornings because I'm
fresh, rested, and generally have no one sending me texts at
that time of day. Sometimes it's helpful to put your cell phone
in another room. Whatever time you choose to spend with God,
be intentional and keep your appointment with Him. Isn't He
more important than a doctor's appointment that you rush to,
ensuring you'll be on time?

> *But whenever you pray, go into your innermost chamber
> and be alone with Father God, praying to him in secret. And
> your Father, who sees all you do, will reward you openly.*
>                                         *Matthew 6:6 TPT*

The SECOND KEY is to **focus your attention on Jesus**. As
a mom of four, I am oftentimes pulled in many different directions, but when one of my children wants to talk to me, they
will interject, "Mom! Look at me!" When our eyes lock, we
begin a two-way conversation. Eye contact is important to
show the person you're engaged with that you are listening.
Let's fix the "eyes" of our hearts on Him, in the stillness of our
time with Him. For some, this may involve physically closing
your eyes.

> *We look away from the natural realm and we fasten our
> gaze onto Jesus who birthed faith within us and who leads
> us forward into faith's perfection.*          *Hebrews 12:2 TPT*

The THIRD KEY is to **pay attention to the spontaneous
thoughts or pictures coming into your mind**. The Father will
call you *son* or *daughter*. He loves to call us Beloved, Child,
Precious One, and so many more endearing names. He gives
pictures and visions (a vision is just a moving picture) in our
minds. He will also speak many scripture verses over you. As

I said in the Introduction, the very first thing I recognized that He was saying to me was from Jeremiah 31:3: *"I love you with an everlasting love."* He weaves scripture with His love; tells you who He is and who you are to Him; convicts your heart and leads you back to righteousness; inspires you to be who He's created you to be; tells you about what He has planned for your future, and so much more. Get ready to experience His goodness, first hand.

> *How precious are your thoughts about me, O God. They cannot be numbered. I can't even count them; they out-number the grains of sand!*     Psalm 139:17-18 NLT

The FOURTH KEY is to **write it down one thought at a time**. No matter if you typically like to write in a journal or not, this goes along with the training. Journaling is a tool to help you in learning to connect with his communication. Not to mention, it would be terrible if the Lord told you some-thing incredibly amazing about your life and then you forgot He'd said it. You may say, "No way! I'd never forget!" That's what I thought, too. But over the years, I have quite a few journals full of His love. I could pick one off my shelf, open to any page that I'd recorded what He was speaking and become totally overwhelmed with emotion. It's easy to forget specifics. He is so good, and He will speak life into us as much as we will make time to listen. Some days I have written multiple pages, and other days, only a few words. Some people receive more pictures and visions and dreams than thoughts in words. Habakkuk said, "I will watch to SEE what he will say to me."

> *I will stand my watch and set myself on the rampart, and **watch to see what He will say to me,** and what I will answer when I am corrected. Then the Lord answered me and said: "Write the **vision** and make it plain on tablets, that he may run who reads it. For the vision is yet for an appointed time; but at the end it will speak, and it will not lie. Though it tarries, wait for it; because it will surely come, it will not tarry."*     Habakkuk 2:1-2 NKJV

In this passage, the Lord shows He values us recording His word/vision to us. But the more time we have for Him, coming near in humility and a teachable spirit, the more we receive. I've known many who prefer to type what they hear coming into their minds and hearts. But whichever way you choose, recording it is an excellent way to hear and steward the rhema word of God.

So, to recap the **four simple keys** to hear God's voice:

1.  Be still and quiet.
2.  Give your attention to Jesus.
3.  Notice the spontaneous thoughts/pictures coming in your mind.
4.  Write the thoughts down as you "hear" them!

## Leave Your Own Agenda at the Door

When you sit with a friend and talk over a cup of coffee, there's something special when your friend asks, with genuine interest, "What's on your heart today?" Or, "Tell me what's going on with you?" Basically, they're asking, "What would you like to talk about?" It makes you realize they love and care about you and your interests. Similarly, when we come to the Father to listen to Him, let's leave our own agenda at the door and ask Him, "What is on your heart today, Lord?" This is how we diligently seek Him and come deeper into the place of "knowing" our Father, Jesus and beloved Holy Spirit.

> *And this is the way to have eternal life — to know you, the only true God, and Jesus Christ, the one you sent to earth.*
> *John 17:3 NLT*

## What If I Record Something That Isn't God?

Everyone has to practice when they begin something new! Don't overthink this thing. It HAS TO BE SIMPLE, or a child couldn't do it, right? Have you ever been around a toddler who's learning to walk? Imagine it. Here he comes... toddling toward you, eyes locked on yours, arms reaching out, there's a big smile on his face... and then his feet get tangled and he trips! He falls down. What do you do as a loving parent? Run over to him, pick him up, and give him the biggest hug EVER. You're not mad... you're proud of him for trying. And then, after you have celebrated him trying, you put him back in position to keep practicing.

> *Jesus said, "You parents – if your children ask for a loaf of bread, do you give them a stone instead? Or if they ask for a fish, do you give them a snake? Of course not! So, if you sinful people know how to give good gifts to your children, how much more will your heavenly Father give good gifts to those who ask him."*  *Matthew 7:9-11 NLT*

Your heavenly Father is your biggest cheerleader. His desire is to connect with you and develop an intimate relationship with every single one of His beloved children. With YOU.

*Chapter 10*

# DIFFERENT WAYS
# YOU CAN HEAR HIM

*A*lthough we were all made to hear the still, small voice of our Father, sometimes people hear him in various methods — according to the Father's creative stamp on each of us. It is so true that he is very creative. Just look around at creation and you will see His level of creativity is crazy amazing. In an intricate manner, He has made each of us so unique and special. It seems that we can hear from the Lord in many different ways, but some people tend to be "wired" toward receiving in a certain capacity. Hearing God is a general way to say receiving communication and connection with Him as He reveals His heart or plans to you. Let's look at some different modes of receiving.

## Five General Ways People Can Hear God

### Hearer

Those who primarily hear God speaking in words usually receive a lot of details and many times record them, so they are not forgotten. They receive a lot of revelation and face the temptation to work independently, instead of in community. Sometimes hearers receive prophetic words for individuals or the corporate body of Christ.

## Seer

Seers hear God and connect with Him through pictures, impressions, visions, or dreams. Sometimes visual learners can receive communication from the Lord in this way. An impression is just a still picture in your mind, while visions are moving pictures—almost like a movie being played out. Visions can be seen with your eyes open or closed. A seer's eyes can be opened to the spiritual realm and see angels and even demons. Dreaming is a common way the Lord speaks as well. If you dream a vivid dream, write it down. I've received a lot of direction from the Lord through my dreams. Ask the Holy Spirit to explain it. He is the best interpreter. Christian dream interpretation books can also help you in determining what your dreams mean.

## Feeler

Feelers have a strong discernment from the Lord and can pick up on feelings of others as well as *feel* the Father's heart for other people. They also receive feelings about what is going on in the atmosphere around them. Many who do not realize they have this gift of discernment will feel like they are on an emotional roller coaster when actually the Father is giving them insight into what is going on in the room so they can be *change agents* and speak life or peace into situations.

## Knower

If you are a knower, you probably know it. They tend to have strong intuition and they just know things. This is usually confirmed after the situation plays out and they were right. Of course, we should constantly be aligning ourselves with the Word of God, not just following our own ways. Somehow, when it comes to being led by God, they know that they know that they know.

Testimony

*Knowing* is similar to a gift of the Holy Spirit called a *word of knowledge*. Once I was talking to a server at a restaurant and had a strong thought that she had pain in her neck. I wanted to ask her if she had the pain, but I chickened out. Thoughts started hitting me that she probably didn't, and she'd think I was weird. I ended up leaving the restaurant without mentioning it. After driving about a mile down the road, the Holy Spirit told me to turn around. In obedience, I very reluctantly turned around, feeling silly to walk back in and ask the server if she had neck pain.

A booming thought in my head was, "What if she thinks I'm crazy?" But I just continued to feel as though the Lord was saying, "Go. I am with you!" So, I went in and asked Jenny if she had neck pain and she said YES! She wondered how I knew. I was able to tell her of the love of Jesus and how He had apprehended me down the road to turn around and pray for her neck pain. I prayed and her pain went from a 9 to a 4. (On a scale of 0-10, 10 being the worst.) I prayed a second time and the pain went completely away. She started to cry because the pain had been pretty constant since her car accident years before.

I found out a few weeks later, from a different server at the restaurant, she had been running from God, but that the encounter with Jesus healing her neck highly impacted her. That day had been a turning point in her life. The reason I had the word of knowledge was to reach her wandering heart and allow Jesus to demonstrate his powerful love. Whew! So thankful I went back. It's really never too late to turn around and walk with God in obedience.

**Talker**

Have you ever known someone who is an outward processor? They process information and situations by talking about them out loud. As they discuss the situation, the more the Lord reveals to their understanding. Often some weighty revelations can come from these moments of verbal discussion.

Some hear and receive from God in several ways, and a few people can experience all of them regularly. Although the primary way I experience revelation is as a HEARER, I have experienced all these ways and you can, too.

## Roadblocks to Hearing God

If you run into a roadblock, don't get frustrated because although it may be TRUE you're having a block, the fact you're not hearing Him doesn't align with TRUTH. The Bible is truth and it says you can connect with your heavenly Father. Try these things:

- Pour your heart out to Him and run to Him in repentance for any sin in your life.

- If you find your mind wandering or thinking furiously of the things you need to remember, make a list of those distracting thoughts. Once you write them down, you can begin to clear your mind without worrying.

- Examine your thinking about who you believe you are in Christ. Lies can bring you into bondage and influence you into believing "It's just not for you," or "God is mad at me," or "I must not have the gift of hearing God." These are lies. As a son or daughter, you are created to hear your Father speak to you. It's not a gift, it's a birthright. Break agreement with the lies you may be believing. (For a sample prayer, see chapter 10.) Read and declare the truth about who you are as a child of God. (Identity scriptures found in Appendix A.)

- Worship Him with a pure heart (not to get something from Him).

- Fasting with right motives can increase our sensitivity to God's voice. (See Appendix C for a suggestion for a great book on fasting.)

## Key Ways to Know it's Him

Maybe hearing Him is not a problem, but maybe you've been wondering how to know for sure it is the Lord. There are a few keys that can help.

- **What you receive should reflect the nature of God and align with His Word.** The Bible says God is love, and this is demonstrated as He speaks. You will also hear scripture "come alive" because He speaks His Word and weaves its meaning into your life. There have been times I've heard him say a phrase to me over and over, later to realize it was a Bible verse. It is so important for us to become beautifully familiar with the Word of God.

- **You will know the source by its fruit.** As you hear and write, does the message produce in you the fruit of the Spirit? Galatians 5:22 says:

  *But the fruit produced by the Holy Spirit within you is divine **love** in all its varied expressions: **joy** that overflows, **peace** that subdues, **patience** that endures, **kindness** in action, a life full of **virtue**, **faith** that prevails, **gentleness** of heart, and strength of spirit. Never set the law above these qualities, for they are meant to be limitless. (TPT)*

  If what you receive produces fear, anxiety, guilt, shame, condemnation, discouragement, inadequacy, or confusion... THIS IS NOT YOUR FATHER.

  God's voice always brings inspiration, life, love, and hope.

- **It's helpful to seek wise counsel from spiritual leaders in your life.** Find several leaders in your life that have a solid orientation with the Word of God and who are familiar with regularly hearing His voice and His guidance. Gaining wisdom and perspective from those who are a few steps ahead of you in the journey of being led by the Spirit of God is an excellent way to walk in accountability and to stay on the right path.

*Chapter 11*

# THE POWER
# OF OUR WORDS

*T*he Bible says there is power in the words we speak. Why is this? God made man in his image (Genesis 1:27). When God speaks, He creates.

> *Then God said, "Let there be light," and there was light.*
> *Genesis 1:3 ESV*

As sons and daughters of God, we are made in His image, and the Bible says our words also have power. This is, in part, how we were created in His image. Our words have the power to build up or destroy. Pay attention to the words you use. Are they filled with criticism, hate, and defeat… or love, hope, and encouragement? They are like tools that can either help us reach our goals or leave us stuck in a deep, dark valley.

> *The **words** of the wicked are like a murderous ambush, but the words of the godly save lives.* Proverbs 12:6 NLT

Speaking life with our words brings life and fruit, but speaking negative words, lies, and criticism can put us in bondage and hold us back from stepping into the destiny that God has dreamed for us. Words are also damaging to others. Look at what Psalm 64:2-3 says:

> *Hide me from the conspiracy of the wicked, from the plots of evildoers. They sharpen their tongues like swords and aim cruel words like deadly arrows. (NIV)*

The words you speak really matter. Look at Jesus says in Matthew 12:34b-37 to the Pharisees:

> *You brood of vipers! How can you speak good, when you are evil? For out of the abundance of the heart the mouth speaks. The good person out of his good treasure brings forth good, and the evil person out of his evil treasure brings forth evil. I tell you, on the day of judgment people will give account for every careless word they speak, for by your words you will be justified, and by your words you will be condemned.*
> *Matthew 12:34-37 ESV*

If you are stuck in a downward spiral of continually criticizing yourself or others, go to God in repentance. Break agreement with coming under a critical spirit and commit to taking these thoughts captive... which is where the criticism and negativity begins, in your mind. When you begin to hear these negative thoughts, recognize your battle is not with flesh and blood enemies, but with the spiritual forces of evil in the heavenly places (Ephesians 6:12). Begin to speak the Word of God over your life because the word is truth and it is alive (Hebrews 4:12). Ask the Father for verses and/or try Googling appropriate scriptures for what you're going through and then stand on it.

According to Isaiah 55:11, God's Word does not return void but accomplishes what He sends it to do.

> *The rain and snow come down from the heavens and stay on the ground to water the earth. They cause the grain to grow, producing seed for the farmer and bread for the hungry. **It is the same with my word. I send it out, and it always produces fruit.** It will accomplish all I want it to, and it will prosper everywhere I send it.*
> *Isaiah 55:10-11 NLT*

When we speak His Word (written or spoken), we know it will accomplish what He sends it to do. His Word is truth and it does not return void. As we speak His Word, things begin to shift in the unseen realm, even though we may not see anything change in the natural at first.

## Speaking It Into Existence

One morning I woke up, and I became conscious of what was playing in my mind over and over. I said it out loud: "CALL INTO BEING THAT WHICH IS NOT YET." I thought, "What is that? I have never heard that phrase before." I wrote it down. A few days later, I found it in the Bible. It is a verse that speaks about Abraham's faith and how God taught him how to believe Him for what He'd promised OVER what his life displayed at the moment!

> *He [Abraham] is our example and father, for in God's presence he believed that God can raise the dead and* **call into being things that don't even exist yet***.*
> *Romans 4:17b TPT*

Abram believed God for a promised child even though he was a hundred years old. God wants us to have faith like Abram and speak out the promises He's given us for our life or the life of the one we are praying for, even when the situation currently looks NOTHING like that promise. God changed Abram's name to Abraham because it meant "Father of many." Did I mention they were WAY too old for children? God called Abraham… "a father of many" into being.

> *When Abram was ninety-nine years old, the Lord appeared to him and said, "I am El-Shaddai – 'God Almighty.' Serve me faithfully and live a blameless life. I will make a covenant with you, by which I will guarantee to give you countless descendants." At this, Abram fell face down on the ground. Then God said to him, "This is my covenant with you: I will make you the father of a multitude of nations! What's more, I am changing your name. It will no longer*

> *be Abram. Instead, you will be called Abraham, for you will*
> *be the father of many nations.*　　*Genesis 17:1-5 NLT*

Our words have power. The Lord calls into being that which is not. This is what we are doing when we STAND ON HIS PROMISES. In my quiet time, the Lord began talking to me about standing on His promises for some things I had been praying about, diligently. He would say, "Daughter, look at me, not your circumstances." "Declare my Word and STAND." Although I saw the opposite of His promise playing out for a member of my family, I continued to say OUT LOUD the promises I had heard the Lord tell me. When you're praying for someone, ask the Lord who they are to Him. Who He created them to be. Or ask Him for a word He wants to speak about the situation. Making sure it is in alignment with His nature and the Word, begin to thank Him for that promise for the person you're praying for.

For example, in faith, thank God for the breakthrough just as if it has already happened. I would say, "Father I thank you that 'Bill' is a mighty man of God! All doubt is crushed in his life and he walks by faith. Thank you, Lord that you are his first love." God is so pleased when we praise him in faith BEFORE the breakthrough.

About two years later, the breakthrough came, just as He said. He is so faithful to perform his word.

> *Then the Lord said to me, "You have seen well, for I am*
> *watching over my word to perform it."*
> 　　　　　　　　　　　　　　　　*Jeremiah 1:12 ESV*

## Decrees

The Word of God says we as the body of Christ are **kings** and **priests**.

> *To Him who loved us and washed us from our sins in His*
> *own blood and has made us **kings** and **priests** to His God*
> *and Father, to Him be glory and dominion forever and ever.*
> *Amen.*　　　　　　　　　　　　*Revelation 1:5b-6 NKJV*

With an understanding that we are called priests and kings, let's look at those in relation to prayer before the Father.

- *Priestly prayer* is connecting to the heart of God through worship and intimacy, and intercession. As disciples of Jesus, our calling looks similar to His in His earthly ministry.

   > *The Spirit of the Lord God is upon Me, because the Lord has anointed Me to preach good tidings to the poor; he has sent Me to heal the brokenhearted, to proclaim liberty to the captives, and the opening of the prison to those who are bound; to proclaim the acceptable year of the Lord, and the day of vengeance of our God; to comfort all who mourn, to console those who mourn in Zion, to give them beauty for ashes, the oil of joy for mourning, the garment of praise for the spirit of heaviness; that they may be called trees of righteousness, the planting of the Lord, that He may be glorified...But you shall be named the **priests of the Lord**, they shall call you the servants of our God.*
   > *Isaiah 61:1-3,6a NKJV*

   > *My sons, do not now be negligent, for the Lord has chosen you to stand in his presence to minister to him, and to be his ministers and make offerings to him.*
   > *2 Chronicles 29:11*

- *Kingly prayer* is using authority given to us by the King of Kings, Jesus Christ, to decree God's Word to move mountains. As kings, we are CONFIDENT OF OUR IDENTITY in Christ and have dominion in the kings' domain (kingdom) to address anything out of order, such as demons or diseases. The kingdom boundaries are established by the Word of God... if the Lord says it, as kings, we enforce it by a decree.

> *So you also are complete through your union with Christ, who is the head over every ruler and authority.*
> *Colossians 2:10 NLT*

> *Behold, I give you the authority to trample on serpents and scorpions, and over all the power of the enemy, and nothing shall by any means hurt you.*
> *Luke 10:19 NKJV*

> *Then Jesus said to the disciples, "Have faith in God. I tell you the truth, you can **say** to this mountain, 'May you be lifted up and thrown into the sea,' and it will happen. But you must really believe it will happen and have no doubt in your heart. I tell you, you can pray for anything, and if you believe that you've received it, it will be yours."*
> *Mark 11:22 NLT*

As Christ's followers, we can decree his word and see the mountains move!

A **decree** is by definition an official order issued by a legal or governmental authority, or to order something by a proclamation. As sons and daughters of God, made in His image, we can speak or decree the Word of God over our lives. It is extremely important that we KNOW our identity in Christ. Speaking His WORD includes the logos word (Bible), as well as the rhema word (spoken word from the Lord).

> *You will also **decree** a thing, and it will be established for you; And light will shine on your ways.*
> *Job 22:28 NASB*

We decree the Word of God. Speak it out loud. Our own opinions do not come into play here. God's will aligns with His Word, and His Word is truth. It's so important that we get the Word of the Lord into our minds and hearts. We must settle it in our hearts that the Word of God is absolute truth. The Bible says: if He says it, He will fulfill it.

*"God is not man, that he should lie, or a son of man, that he should change his mind. Has he said, and will he not do it? Or has he spoken, and will he not fulfill it?"*
*Numbers 23:19 ESV*

We will begin to see miracles manifest when we pray, decree, and never give up. Faith is standing on the Word of God and trusting His word MORE than what we see in the natural.

## Testimony of the Power of the Decree

A short time back, my husband and I signed up to go on a mission trip to Colombia, South America. The trip was set for February. My husband is a dentist by trade and, in that line of work, January is typically slow for his business. Thankfully, we had already paid the cost of the trip for the two of us in advance. But, as Christmas passed and January came, business was very slow. Many patients were cancelling because of sickness and Christmas debts. My husband began to warn me that if things didn't pick up around the office, there was no way he'd be able to go on the trip. When he isn't working, the office has to close because he is the only dentist.

So I began to decree God's blessings and provision over his dental office. I began to decree the word over the situation: "John 10:10 says even though the thief comes only to steal kill and destroy, JESUS, you come to give us life, abundantly. I decree abundant life and provision and patients bursting at the seams. I thank you, God for walk-in patients, call-in patients, and paying patients. Thank you for abundant provision, Lord."

I prayed this kingly prayer in my secret place for three to four days. On the fifth day, I went into the office to take something to my husband. The receptionist motioned me over to her desk. She leaned in to ask me a question. "Ashley, have you been praying by any chance for increase?" I giggled and asked why she asked. She told me that morning something had *let loose.* They'd had patients calling on the phone all day, walking in the door needing to be seen, and the day's mail brought many outstanding payments. Her eyes were as big as saucers. I began to explain how I had been decreeing and declaring the promise of God's provision over the office and praying for an increase in business so he could close the office and go on the mission trip.

TO GOD BE THE GLORY. We went and saw the Lord move in lives and hearts in mighty ways, including our own. Breakthrough doesn't come that fast every time... but it will come if you don't give up.

## Believe and Speak Identity

Understanding and believing your identity in Christ is an extremely important thing in the Christian faith. Speak the truth of your identity over yourself and over each member of your family. Tell your children who God says they are, even if they don't act like it. I tell my teenage boys that they are "mighty men of God with great faith." The first few times I said it, I got the *raised eyebrow look*, but now they just smile. One day the Lord was speaking to me and He said,

> *"Beloved, speak over them who they are and they'll begin to come into agreement with it as well. Pound them with how they fall short, and they'll live in shame and condemnation. If the body of Christ will come into agreement with My Word about their identity and how Christ died for them to be as sons and daughters, things will shift. Words have power. Tell people who they ARE, not who they're NOT. SPEAK LIFE."*

*Chapter 12*

# THE GREAT COMMISSION IS FOR EVERYONE

*And Jesus came and said to them, "All authority in heaven*
*and on earth has been given to me.* **Go therefore and make**
**disciples of all nations, baptizing them in the name**
**of the Father and of the Son and of the Holy Spirit,**
**and teaching them to obey everything that I have**
**commanded you.** *And remember, I am with you always,*
*to the end of the age.*
*Matthew 28:18-20 NRSV*

*H*ave you ever been in love? Being in love sometimes causes us to do passionate things we may not normally do. That might be anything from driving across town just to put a note on that someone's car, to making a great personal sacrifice for that person. With LOVE there is sacrifice. Look at the sacrifice God himself made in the giving of Jesus to lay His life down for you and me. Jesus said:

> *For the greatest love of all is a love that sacrifices all. And*
> *this great love is demonstrated when a person sacrifices his*
> *life for his friends.*        *John 15:13 TPT*

Jesus didn't just *say* He loved us. He lived it. He came to demonstrate the Father's immense love for us. He suffered for this love. At any moment, He could've called 10,000 angels to get Him off that cross. But *love* kept Him there. That, my friends, is true love. For YOU. Hebrews chapter 12 says that He endured that cross because of the JOY set before Him. The joy of gaining YOU as part of His bride.

> *And let us run with perseverance the race marked out for us,*
> *fixing our eyes on Jesus, the pioneer and perfecter of faith.*
> *For the **joy** set before him he endured the cross, scorning its*
> *shame, and sat down at the right hand of the throne of God.*
> *Hebrews 12:1b-2 NIV*

This level of love and sacrifice demands a response from those being rescued. How do you respond? As we walk with Jesus daily, hearing His voice of truth, speaking love, hope, and inspiration over us; we begin to *know* this LOVE. We begin to trust this love. In this safe place of confidence in our Father's love, we begin to hear Jesus say, "Follow Me." Because God's heart is for all to come to repentance and enter into His family, He needs all of his sons and daughters to join hands and reach those who remain lost.

In the past, many believers have titled those that reach the lost "evangelists." But let's look at it from a different perspective. This intimate relationship we have with our Savior and Bridegroom creates in our heart deep, passionate love. When someone is in love, they are willing to sacrifice. Would you be willing to tell everyone you meet about an amazing love that has gripped your heart? What if "laying our life down for our friends" looks like stepping out of your comfort zone to share the good news of the gospel with someone? Could you lay aside your personal agenda for a particular moment for a special assignment from Jesus to love someone who is hurting and desperate for hope, even in the supermarket? You don't have to fit the mold of how you've seen or even imagined this done before. The truth is, Jesus wants you to just be you. Let His love and kindness flow from your lips and tell the person how much He loves them and how He gave his life for them. There are five little words that connect heaven to earth for miracles. Any guesses? *Can. I. Pray. For. You.*

Shortly after I began hearing the voice of God and diligently recording what I was hearing Him say, I became inspired to love strangers and pray for those with physical needs. I had never considered doing this before. I began learning about His desire to reach hearts with authentic miracles... by healing their bodies and touching their hearts with prophetic words. He is a Father who loves to bestow radical kindness, generosity, and love. As they taste and see that He is good, many are so overwhelmed that they are positioned to accept the invitation from the Savior for rescue and to offer a commitment of their life to his love.

## Declaration and Demonstration

Jesus taught his disciples to not only *declare* the gospel but also *demonstrate* it. When He sent out the twelve disciples to reach the lost, He said:

> *As you go, proclaim this message: 'The kingdom of heaven has come near.' Heal the sick, raise the dead, cleanse those who have leprosy, drive out demons. Freely you have received; freely give.*        *Matthew 10:8 NIV*

Later he sent out seventy-two additional men and said:

> *"And heal the sick there, and say to them, 'The kingdom of God has come near to you.'"*        *Luke 10:9 NKJV*

Jesus modeled everything before He asked them to do as He did. Notice He *didn't* say, "Go forth and preach about Me and when I come to those places, I'll show them miracles." No. He told His guys to go declare the kingdom and demonstrate it with His love and power.

Daniel Kolenda, a missionary-evangelist for Christ for All Nations, has led over twenty-one-million lost people to Jesus at crusades in open-air fields in Africa and other places. They frequently see thousands healed and delivered when the gospel is preached. Wheelchairs are held in the air as the paralyzed walk and the blind see. Even the dead have been raised. He was interviewed in the Christian documentary film, [5]"The Finger of God 2," and said, "Jesus didn't heal the sick to prove that He could, He healed the sick to prove that WE could. He did miracles to show us how we can live our lives."

This is how the apostle Paul went about in those early days as the church began. Look at what he says in Romans 15:18-19:

> *I will not venture to speak of anything except what Christ has accomplished through me in leading the Gentiles to obey God by what I have said and done — by the power of signs and wonders, through the power of the Spirit of God. So from Jerusalem all the way around to Illyricum, I have fully proclaimed the gospel of Christ. NIV*

In these verses, Paul gives Jesus glory for his accomplishments in leading the lost to Him. He says he proclaimed the full Gospel by what he SAID AND DID. What did he do? Signs, wonders, and miracles through the power of the Holy Spirit. Again, he not only declared, he demonstrated. In his letter to Corinth, he talks about the Gospel and its power.

> *For the kingdom realm of God comes with power, not simply impressive words.*            *1 Corinthians 4:20 TPT*

## Making Disciples

First, let's talk about what the word *disciple* means. The Cambridge Dictionary defines disciple as "a person who believes in the ideas and principles of someone famous and tries to live the way that person does or did."[6] We see this with Jesus' disciples. They followed Him, learned from Him, and committed themselves to do what He did. Jesus told them to "make disciples...teaching them to obey all the commands I have given you." (Matt. 28:19-20). The disciples were to pass on ALL that Jesus taught them. We can't pick and choose what Jesus meant here. One cannot deny that the Bible gives much attention to Jesus teaching the disciples (among others) to demonstrate the Gospel with miracles and proclaim the kingdom of God had come near. Quite a few generations have passed since then, but WE are His disciples for today. We are called to continue to make disciples until the whole world hears.

> *Yet through it all, this joyful assurance of the realm of heaven's kingdom will be proclaimed all over the world, providing every nation with a demonstration of the reality of God. And after this the end of this age will arrive.*
> *Matthew 24:14 TPT*

The Bible says Jesus came to represent the Father. Similarly, as the body of Christ, we are called to represent Jesus to the world. Jesus prayed for OUR generation of disciples the night before He died:

> *Just as you sent me into the world, I am sending them into the world. And I give myself as a holy sacrifice for them so they can be made holy by your truth. I am praying not only for these disciples but also for all who will ever believe in me through their message.*          *John 17:18 NLT*

That is us, friends. 2 Corinthians 5:20 calls us *Ambassadors for Christ*. An ambassador is a representative of someone or something. Jesus said He is sending us into the world to represent Him and reconcile people to Him.

> *...God was in Christ reconciling the world to Himself, not counting people's sins against them [but canceling them]. And He has committed to us the message of reconciliation [that is, restoration to favor with God]. So we are ambassadors for Christ, as though God were making His appeal through us; we [as Christ's representatives] plead with you on behalf of Christ to be reconciled to God.*
> *2 Corinthians 5:19-20 AMP*

## As You Go, Be Ambassadors for Jesus

My husband Shawn and I were on our way home from a Power and Love conference that took place in Dallas, Texas in 2017. On the plane, Shawn sat by a guy named Justin (I changed his name for privacy). They began to talk and realized they had a lot in common. When he asked why we were in Dallas, Shawn got to share about the conference. Justin admitted he was a believer but had been "lukewarm" in his walk with God. Shawn began to share truth about his identity in Christ, sonship, and testimonies of how we were able to put the gospel on display that week, as we loved people every place we went. Many we prayed for were healed!

Justin immediately said, "Can you pray for me? I have a ton of back pain." Shawn laid his hand on his back and prayed in Jesus' name for healing. His back got extremely cold like there was an ice pack on it, and ALL THE PAIN LEFT. He looked shocked. He felt Shawn's hand to see if it was cold like his back, and Shawn said "Dude, it's not me! It's Jesus!" As they continued to talk, Shawn shared his story and told him how he'd personally been radically changed by the love of Christ. He prayed for him and the Holy Spirit's presence lavished Justin with Jesus' tangible love right there on the plane. They exchanged phone numbers and he later texted Shawn to thank him for his obedience. He said the encounter with God had changed his life!

We are ambassadors everywhere we go. You alone may not change the whole world, but you can change the world for one.

## Representing Jesus

What does it look like to represent Jesus practically in our lives?

- LOVE

  When we are being filled up every day in the secret place as we listen to the voice of the Father, we become filled to the point of overflow with the love of God. It is from the overflow in our own lives that we can freely give love everywhere we go.

*Let all that you do be done in love.*
*1 Corinthians 16:14 NASB*

Love in action speaks much louder than just words. It might manifest itself as: Communicating to people that they are valuable to God through eye contact and a smile. You could start a conversation with someone and ask to pray for them in some way. You can tell them how much they are loved by Jesus. You can bring a meal to someone in need or offer to serve them in some way at their home. This communicates genuine love and kindness. Help others without expecting anything in return. Respond with love to someone who is angry with you. Our goal is to shine the love of Jesus into every conversation of our day. His love touches every facet of our life. Freely we have received, so freely we should give.

> *Beloved children, our love can't be an abstract theory we only talk about, but a way of life demonstrated through our loving deeds.*     *1 John 3:18 TPT*

• KINDNESS AND GENEROSITY

What would it look like in our cities if every believer poured out radical kindness and radical generosity everywhere they went? Sometimes, this requires us to take our eyes off ourselves and our personal schedules. Money speaks loudly when we are generous. Leave a BIG tip when you go out to eat! Trusting God is taken to a new level when we don't feel we have extra, yet we give!

Todd White, who has a ministry called Lifestyle Christianity, says his family always leaves a tip to match the price of the bill. This type of radical generosity gets people's attention. Pay for someone's order behind you in the drive through, or in line inside a restaurant or even in a grocery store. Try this... before you go into

Walmart or another shopping area, stop and pray, "Lord, use me to represent you to someone who needs to know you in this store." There are hurting, broken people everywhere that need to see the love of God in action.

One time, I was in Walmart, and I had gotten a full cart of groceries for my family of six. I was looking for an open cashier to check out. One employee flagged me down in the twenty-items-or-less aisle and said he'd be happy to help me since he had no customers. So I agreed and we began loading my food onto the counter. As we worked, I turned and noticed there was a man, woman, and child behind me watching me intently. The woman seemed pretty mad.

Then she spoke up and said, "You know you're in the twenty-items-or-less line!"

I apologized as nicely as I could as she snarled at me. I chose not to mention the offer I had received from the cashier.

Again I said, "I'm sorry, ma'am!"

With all the anger she could muster, she said, "YOU ARE SORRY!" To the cashier, she continued, "You know, I know the manager of this store and I intend to have your job." She kept on and on with the threats, making the young man behind the register very nervous.

I felt my temperature rising. I thought, "Lord, what do I do?" As he began scanning my last few things, I felt Jesus tell me to love her. He's so good. I knew it wasn't my idea... my blood pressure was about to hit the roof. But with the love the Lord had so graciously poured into me that morning, I began to give it away. I turned to her and took the blame for the mistake of getting in the incorrect line. I apologized genuinely. I smiled and looked into her eyes and her husband's eyes, too. I said,

"Ma'am, could I purchase the things you are buying today? I would love to bless you. Jesus loves you and your family so much."

She looked at me, shocked, and said, "Well sure, okay." I turned to her toddler and began talking sweetly to her. She reached up to give me a hug.

As the cashier rang up their items on my tab, the husband looked at me with deep thanks in his eyes. He thanked me and told me he'd be praying for God to return the blessing. The hate on the woman's face became a smile. She gave me a big hug and said, "God bless you." The boy behind the register had a look of utter disbelief. He had just witnessed Jesus in action through a willing heart. And Christ's love always wins.

- HEALING AND PROPHECY

When my friend and I were just learning about power evangelism, we'd go shopping together, and we'd pay close attention to those who may need a touch from Jesus. If we saw someone with a cane or wheelchair, we'd simply walk over and begin a casual conversation. I'd usually ask them how I could pray for them. As I was praying for Jesus to heal their body, my friend would hear from Holy Spirit a prophetic word of love straight from the Father's heart. Sometimes, the person would receive physical healing and God's love through prophecy. Prophecy is a demonstration of love and compassion of the Father's heart to an individual. It unlocks their heart to believe God sees them and encourages and builds them up.

> *"But the one who prophesies speaks to people for their strengthening, encouraging and comfort.*
> *1 Corinthians 14:3 NIV*

Let me tell you of an example of a prophetic word from the Father's heart to mine that I will never forget. I was at a Global Awakening conference last year. I was on the prayer team because I had completed a Physical Healing Certification Course online through Global Awakening. I was praying for a sweet couple who had been struggling with infertility for the past nine years.

After we prayed, the woman grabbed my hand and said, "Do you have a L-shaped porch on the back of your house? And part of the porch is screened in? Is your kitchen and eating area situated beside the porches?"

I stared at her, in utter amazement, as she described my home exactly. I did not know this woman. What she said next really got me.

"You sit with the Father on the screened-in porch, don't you? The Lord just showed me a picture of you sitting with Him on your porch... as He fully delights in you. Oh, my gracious, how He loves you!"

*Wow.* I felt so adored and loved by my Daddy in heaven. My heart skipped a beat as He demonstrated His love for me through my new friend. Through it, I got to experience the reality of God's heart for ME. I felt so treasured by Him.

## Power Evangelism

This is a term that defines one way that many use to share the Gospel with people. In power evangelism, you let Jesus introduce himself to people and demonstrate His love in a tangible way through the power of the Holy Spirit—using you. This could be through healing or prophecy or simply a laying on of a hand on their shoulder and asking Holy Spirit to love them with His tangible presence. It uses the idea previously mentioned of not only declaration but *demonstration*.

John Wimber wrote a book with Kevin Springer called, *Power Evangelism,* in 1986. "The premise of this book is that scripture teaches that power evangelism — the proclamation and supernatural demonstration of the Kingdom of God — is the most effective way of winning followers to Christ."[7] In 2006, a survey was taken from Christianity Today that showed this book came in 12th out of 50 books that were considered the most influential books for evangelicals.

Displaying God's love and power in miracles, signs and wonders is how Jesus himself demonstrated the reality of who He was to the people. He moved in sync with the Holy Spirit and the Father. As yielded children of God, we can "follow Him" by doing the same...giving all the glory to Jesus.

## A Power Evangelism Testimony

One day, my two daughters and I met my mom for dinner. As we tried to decide where to go, I thought to God, "Lord, where should we go?" My next thought was an Asian restaurant called P.F. Chang's. So off we went. Our server was a sweet girl named Ally (not her real name). We small talked a little bit with her, and as she walked away from the table, I felt like she had a headache. Not because she acted like it, I just thought she did. When she returned, I asked her about it, and she said *yes*. She asked me how I knew.

I explained how sometimes God tells me things. I knew if He revealed it, He would heal it. (This is called a word of knowledge in 1 Corinthians 12:8.) I told her God wanted to heal her headache. She let me pray for her when she came back around, and the headache totally left — instantly. Jesus was pursuing her heart. She disappeared, then came back with tears in her eyes and explained, she had been asking God to show her if he was real... that very day.

Now, this. A miracle. I invited her to come to church with me the next day, and she agreed. She not only came, but she gave her life to Jesus. All glory to God! For more information about how to pray for healing, see Appendix C for book and video recommendations.

# An Encounter with God at Sam's Club

I think it's important for us to realize that sharing the love of Jesus doesn't have to take extravagant amounts of time. I was in Sam's club, and I had just checked out. I was walking toward the door with my receipt in hand. There is always an attendant to look at your receipt and match it to the items you purchased.

As I approached the man, with a smile, I said, "Hello sir. How are you feeling today?"

He returned with, "Better now."

When I inquired, he quickly said he'd had a few seizures recently and had caused him some health problems.

I asked, "May I pray for you?" He said sure. I asked Jesus to come love on him and touch his body with His healing presence. Very simple and short. When I looked at him, he had a tear running down each cheek. The Holy Spirit lavished him with His manifest presence right there in Sam's. He was so moved. He thanked me. I saw him about six to eight months later and he'd been free of seizures since the day I'd prayed for him. God is so good. The entire conversation and prayer took less than a minute.

I try and be mindful of people behind me, so I don't get the employee I'm trying to bless in trouble. But it is truly amazing to see how God arranges situations so we can bless others. God doesn't ask us to be perfect professionals, just available and willing to love.

## Is Healing a Gift?

Maybe you're thinking that "you don't have the gift of healing... isn't that a gift only some get?" Actually, yes and no. If you are a true believer in Jesus, healing is a part of your inheritance as a child of the God of the universe. This is Mark's version of *the Great Commission* that we've been looking at in this chapter.

> *And then he told them, "Go into all the world and preach the Good News to everyone. Anyone who believes and is*

*baptized will be saved. But anyone who refuses to believe will be condemned. These miraculous signs will accompany those who believe: They will cast out demons in my name, and they will speak in new languages. They will be able to handle snakes with safety, and if they drink anything poisonous, it won't hurt them. They will be able to place their hands on the sick, and they will be healed."*

*Mark 16:15-18 NLT*

Here we see Jesus declaring everyone should share the good news and then expect signs, wonders, and miracles to follow THOSE WHO BELIEVE. Are you a believer?

In the Book of John, we see Jesus say something unimaginable. He says those coming after him who believe will do even greater works than him.

*I tell you this timeless truth: The person who follows me in faith, believing in me, will do the same mighty miracles that I do – even greater miracles than these because I go to be with my Father!*                 *John 14:12 TPT*

Notice he didn't say those with a gift of healing will do greater miracles. No. The person who believes in him. Randy Clark is the founder of Global Awakening and wrote a book called [8]*The Biblical Basis for Healing*. He speaks about how all Christians are commissioned to heal the sick, and looks at the passage of Matthew 28:19-20:

*This passage is for us just as much as it was for the people of Jesus' day. We are to receive the teachings of Jesus then pass them on to others. Part of the teachings of Jesus include healing and deliverance. The ministry of Jesus was not relegated to the forgiveness of sins. It was to bring healing to the total person – body, soul and spirit. If it doesn't bring freedom to all of these areas, then it is not the same gospel that Jesus preached and demonstrated while He walked on this earth. Did you know you have been commissioned?*

What does the Bible say about the **gift of healing**? In 1 Corinthians 12:7-11, Paul speaks of the Holy Spirit giving the body of Christ supernatural gifts. In verse 9, it mentions the gift of healing. There are special gifts given to people as they encounter people with a certain need. This could also be referring to some individuals having a stronger anointing for healing, based on what the Lord calls them to do in their life. But this doesn't negate the many other scriptures that speak of miracles and wonders following those who believe. I think we can say it is "both/and," not "either/or." The Holy Spirit knows all things and we can trust him to give us gifts beneficial for ministering to others when we give him our availability.

## Conclusion

Jesus walked constantly in fellowship with the Father through the person of the Holy Spirit. We are invited to do the same. The Holy Spirit will lead us, showing us how to love each person we encounter *individually…* just like Jesus did. We are the *body of Christ*. Each one of us is a very important part of a whole. If we would ALL walk in love and follow God's teachings, as His dear children, praying for the sick and seeing them healed and delivered… giving all the glory to God — people would supernaturally experience the gospel as in the book of Acts.

It wouldn't just be fancy or impressive words, but the power of God, pursuing hearts to bring a demonstration of the love of the Father. As we represent Jesus, we must walk in holiness and purity. We've been made into brand-new creations. Throw off sin patterns that are no longer who you are. You are a child of the Most High God. Let's go forward with our eyes set on Jesus — taking every thought captive — making them obedient to our righteous King. Spend time with Him in your secret place and learn what it means to have full communion with him. Intimacy is the KEY. Let's ask the Father to help us become the Word we read and to walk in love everywhere we set our feet to go.

*Be imitators of God in everything you do, for then you will represent your Father as his beloved sons and daughters. And continue to walk surrendered to the extravagant love of Christ, for he surrendered his life as a sacrifice for us. His great love for us was pleasing to God, like an aroma of adoration – a sweet healing fragrance.*

*Ephesians 5:1 TPT*

*Chapter 13*

# GIVE THE GIFT OF YOUR TIME

"The bad news is, TIME FLIES. The good news is,
YOU'RE THE PILOT." -Anonymous

*O*ur time is important to us. How you use it shows your priorities in life. Just about the only thing more valuable than our time is who we spend it with. How important is hearing God speak life, love, and His direction over you? If you will make *seeking* Him a priority in your life, YOU WILL HEAR HIS VOICE, and your life will be transformed. All it takes is a commitment to giving HIM your time. God rewards those who draw near to Him and diligently seek him.

> *"And without faith it is impossible to please him, for who-*
> *ever would draw near to God must believe that he exists*
> *and that he rewards those who seek him."*
> *Hebrews 11:6 ESV*

I've heard people say, "He doesn't talk to me like He talks to you." Hearing God is relative to the amount of time you give Him to speak. We are ALL his favorites. If we gave Him half the time we give to Facebook, Instagram, or Snapchat, we would go forward with God in leaps and bounds.

Likewise, if you want to train to be good at a sport, you know you have to put in the amount of time it takes to practice. The more time you give to practice, the better you become at the sport. Hearing the Lord follows the same principle. Giving him your time is an expression of humility. It's saying, "Knowing

You is important to me, Father, and I will show You with my time!" Making time with Him a priority, we enthrone Him in our lives and dethrone ourselves.

If you don't have a quiet time with God as a part of your routine already, there is no time like the present to begin. Start with an achievable amount of time. Years ago, I started with ten minutes and pretty quickly worked up to thirty minutes. I started realizing how refreshed and renewed spending time with God made me feel… and that was before I knew He wanted to speak to me. I do encourage you to begin to increase your current time with Him, whatever it may be. He rewards those who seek Him by giving grace in the secret place. If thirty minutes seems long, give it a chance. Don't quit. I felt like that in the beginning. But now, if I have the opportunity to sit with him for three hours on the weekends, it goes by so fast it feels like twenty minutes. Also, consider getting up earlier in the mornings to seek Him. I know not everyone is a morning person, but there is something special about you giving him the first fruits of your day. (Just like tithing should come out of your paycheck first, it's the first fruits given to God. For more on first fruits, see Deut. 18:4 and Matt. 6:33) Ask God to help you. He gives rest, joy, and peace when there is none.

As you honor God with your time every day, don't be discouraged if you oversleep or get interrupted; there may be instances that cause you to miss a day or have your time cut short. The enemy may put self-condemning thoughts in your mind, or thoughts that God is displeased with you. Take them captive. Get right back into His presence as soon as possible and know He welcomes you always. His Spirit's conviction draws you back into His loving arms; He never ever pushes you away. Sometimes, we notice a war fighting for our time with the Lord, because the enemy is scared of our intimacy with God. The way we fight back is to never give up. Keep spending time with the Lord, no matter what tries to distract you.

Heidi Baker is an American missionary in Mozambique, Africa—one of the poorest areas of the world. God sent her there and she began to rescue children out of a giant trash dump. Now her ministry has grown to unbelievable proportions. She frequently is witness to God multiplying food, opening deaf ears, and raising the dead.

She said something at a conference that stuck with me. She said, "If you don't quit, YOU WIN!" This is so true. Be diligent. Persevere. Make time for the King of kings to speak to you. As I said earlier, we make priorities for doctor appointments and we make sure to be on time. How important is the Lord of Glory to you? He is the GREAT PHYSICIAN. The amount of time we spend with someone is living proof of our love. Will you give Jesus, your "knight in shining armor", the gift of your TIME?

As I was finishing up the writing of this book, one morning the Father began speaking to me about His sons and daughters hearing His voice. I felt He wanted me to include it here as I close PART ONE:

*All my sons and daughters can hear My voice. I speak to My children differently, according to how I created them, but just as everyone can receive thoughts and temptations from the enemy, they also receive thoughts and directives from Me too. They only need to learn to recognize it's Me. I am good and I desire relationship. Would I allow the devil to speak in a way that I don't? He is the copier. I AM THE ORIGINAL. Stand on My promise that I speak to all who will open their hearts and listen. Align yourself with the truth of My Word, and you will hear Me speaking love and identity over you. I will give the same love that I gave to David. He was a man after My own heart because he was transformed by listening to My heart through My voice. AND he gave Me his time."*

*Part Two*

# 90 DAILY DEVOTIONS AND ACTIVATIONS

Part Two:

# DAILY DEVOTIONS AND ACTIVATIONS

---

*I*n PART TWO of this book, I have compiled ninety daily devotions and activations for you to begin to recognize God's voice and be activated to hear Him speak into your own life. I've taken exact excerpts from my journals that the Lord spoke to me of timeless truths for the body of Christ... you. I asked the Father to lead me to the content He wanted me to include in each daily devotion. From each excerpt, I listed a daily verse as well as scripture references that I noticed God was speaking from in His Word each day. Remember, God always speaks His Word. *I encourage you to look up the references and see how what He says is connected with Scripture. This is how we keep our feet on the Rock and know it is our Daddy speaking.*

After each rhema word from the Lord, I have several declarations and decrees for each day that I encourage you to speak out loud as you stand on the truth of the Word of God for your life. (And feel free to add more of your own.) Remember, our words have power. When we believe what God says about us OVER what we are seeing with our eyes, it's called FAITH. Call into being that which is not yet.

Lastly, I have included a blank page each day for activation. THIS IS THE MOST IMPORTANT PART. Please don't simply read each devotion and stop. God has a NOW WORD for you. For YOU. He has so much to tell you.

Remember, if you don't quit, you win. The reason He asked me to write this book (it was not my idea) was to teach His precious sons and daughters to *hear* Him. He is going to speak to you. He's just waiting on you to listen. Bring Him your time. Bring Him your EXPECTATION. Bring Him your love and adoration.

You will experience the Voice of Truth.

# Day 1: I Love You

"I have loved you with an everlasting love; therefore, with
loving-kindness I have drawn you and have continued
my faithfulness to you." Jeremiah 31:3b AMP

**Psalm 46:10, Psalm 23:4, Isaiah 46:4, John 15:1-17,
Matthew 17:20, Psalm 91:1-2, Romans 8:38-39**

Oh, my beloved one, yes, of course, you can hear me. I
am constantly speaking to you all the time. My love for you
is wild! Choose to believe Me instead of the lies that present
themselves to you as your own thoughts. I will lead you down
the path of truth. Be still and know me. Put your phone down
more. It is good technology, but also a heavy distraction. Full
communion with Me needs space. Sit with Me in the quiet. I
will reveal secrets as you make Me your focus. I am so pleased
you are discovering the truth about your identity. We are on a
journey. Sometimes there are hills and mountains where the
view is exciting and takes your breath away. But in the valley,
you are transformed. I am in both places with you. Especially
the valleys. Your testimony of healing from lies believed will
help you in helping others.

Let's walk together closely. Hold my hand, beloved. Don't
look around... look at me. I will sustain you when you are
hungry. I will give you living water when you're thirsty. I am
enough. Come to the river and let me refresh your soul. Abide
in Me, my love. Press into what it means to abide. Begin to
decree and declare things over your life and your family. Your
words shift atmospheres. I can move mountains through the
lips of my faithful ones. You are the one my heart adores. Stand.
Stand up and bask in this love I lavish on you freely. You are
pure and righteous in my sight... justified because My Beloved
Son laid his life down for you. You are chosen. Rejoice in My
love, my child! You have no grid for the joy that awaits you in
my presence. I never change. I love to love you. Come sit right
beside me—in my shadow. You are mine! Do you understand
what this means? No one anywhere can separate you from My
love. You are My treasure!

## Declarations and Decrees of Truth

I decree and declare that I am a child of God, made pure and righteous by the blood of Jesus.
I decree and declare that my thoughts are now subject to the Lordship of Jesus Christ.

_____

_____

_____

_____

_____

_____

_____

_____

_____

_____

_____

_____

_____

_____

_____

# Day 2: You've Been Made Pure and Righteous

"And there is still much more to say of his unfailing love for us! For through the blood of Jesus we have heard the powerful declaration, "You are now righteous in my sight. And because of the sacrifice of Jesus, you will never experience the wrath of God." Romans 5:9 TPT

**Revelation 22:1-2, Romans 4:17, John 15:9-11, 2 Corinthians 5:21, 2 Corinthians 10:5, Hebrews 9:12, Titus 2:14**

My beloved child, I meet you right where you are. Always. Dear one, come to the edge of the river with Me. The River of God in My throne room is living and makes you fully alive. It and the tree of life are for life and healing. Just like My Word. Meditate on My Word and speak it out. Call into being that which is not yet. Abide in Me. Abiding is resting in who I AM. It is the opposite of striving. Trust Me in everything. Talk to Me about everything—choices, decisions, excitement, despair. Ask Me, beloved. Bring all of you. My wisdom flows to those who sit in the fear of the Lord with humble hearts. I gaze at you. I NEVER let you out of my sight. Many would be intimidated by this truth, but let it spur you on to more purity and holiness. You have been made righteous. You are justified. Freed from the bondage of sin. So walk like it. My Spirit in you gives you strength and helps you take the temptations captive and makes them obedient to Me. This is the WAY. My blood speaks a better word than the blood of bulls and goats. (Hebrews 9:12) I AM your Redeemer.

## Declarations and Decrees of Truth

I decree and declare that my past will not dictate my future.
I decree and declare that Jesus is Lord and King over my life.
I decree and declare that my life will exemplify humility, honesty, compassion, and honor.

# Day 3: Do Not Fear

"God is love, and whoever abides in love, abides
in God and God abides in him… There is no fear
in love, but perfect love casts out fear."
1 John 4:16b, 18a NASB

**Isaiah 41:10, Isaiah 26:3, Deuteronomy 31:6, Psalm 124:8,
Psalm 16:5, 2 Corinthians 5:20, Hebrews 12:1-2, John 10:3-4**

Beloved, I run to you as your defender. I am the Lord of Hosts. Do not fear. My perfect overshadowing love casts fear away from you as it draws you closer to Me. You must know that fear is an ILLUSION. The enemy sometimes throws his own fear on you, which is a feeling many think is their own. This turns into worry. Neither of these are your portion. I AM your portion and I am your strength. As My child, you are able to rise up above any situation. Look into My eyes and you will see My love and kindness and power wrapping around you. I am greater than any situation you find yourself in. Don't believe the enemy when you get the idea that My hands are tied. You are My ambassador and all of Heaven backs you up. You have a cloud of witnesses... so run this race with endurance and perseverance — using My strength. You are never alone. Just close your eyes and you will see My face. I will be with you, My beloved one. You are Mine by choice. I chose you for this great harvest. This is a momentous season. Listen to My voice and My Word and obey. Honor and love others and live this gospel. Let people be influenced by your life lived. And remember, you never walk alone. I love you more than your human heart can take in. So trust Me. THIS LOVE is yours.

## Declarations and Decrees of Truth

I decree and declare that I will walk in truth and not in error.
I decree and declare that God's protection will keep me from harm.
I decree and declare that the angels of the Lord are fighting for me.
I decree and declare that I will not be anxious about anything, because Jesus lives in me.

# DAY 4: HAVE FAITH BEYOND YOUR SIGHT

"To have faith is to be sure of the things we hope for, to be certain of the things we cannot see." Hebrews 11:1 GNT

**Psalm 23:5, Psalm 91:11-12, Genesis 1:26-28, Romans 4:17,
2 Corinthians 5:20, John 8:44, Luke 10:19, 2 Corinthians 10:5,
John 3:19-21, Psalms 8:6-8, Nehemiah 8:10**

My love for you stretches beyond your understanding. And My timing is perfect... you will see. Keep your eyes on Me. I prepare a table for you in the presence of your enemies. We can commune together no matter what or who is trying to bring you down. I will hold you up. I am your defender—the Lord of Hosts. I will command My angels concerning you and your family. At My name, the darkness trembles. I reward those who earnestly seek Me, regardless of what they actually see with their eyes. Faith is BELIEVING WHEN YOU DO NOT SEE. I am equipping you to trust Me when you see the opposite of what I have said. I raise the dead to life. I call into being that which is not yet. What I say goes and I say you will be My mighty ambassador who carries My authority and power and love into the darkness. My plans will succeed... I have seen it. Everything you hear from the enemy is a lie. He is the father of lies. Do not believe your feelings. BELIEVE ME. Declare what I have said over yourself. Speak it out and watch it come into being. This is because you are My child and you have been given dominion over the earth and authority over all the enemy's schemes. Take your thoughts captive—examine them and throw them into the light to see if they are truth. Truth likes the light but lies run. Practice this mindfully every day, starting today. I will help you, beloved. You are Mine. Stand in your identity. Do not back down. The darkness trembles at My name. My promises will come to pass... you can stand on them. Make My JOY your strength!

## Declarations and Decrees of Truth

I decree and declare I am part of a chosen race, a royal priesthood, a holy nation, and a people for God's own possession.

I decree and declare I am an heir of God and a joint-heir with Jesus Christ.

I decree and declare I am an ambassador carrying Christ's authority, power, and love.

# DAY 5: ABIDE

"If you abide in me and my words abide in you, ask whatever you wish and it will be done for you... As the Father
has loved me, so have I loved you. Abide in my love."
John 15:7, 9 NRSV

**Proverbs 18:21, Psalm 46:10, Luke 11:9, Proverbs 3:5,6, Zephaniah
3:17, Deuteronomy 30:20, Isaiah 30:21, Isaiah 50:4, John 10:27**

My beautiful child, My heart pours love over you. I see
you and I delight in you. I see you are learning to abide. More
beloved, abide more. Connect your thoughts with Mine. The
more time we spend together, the closer we become. Begin to
speak and declare truth over yourself, your family and situations. "Be still and know me" more. Ask to receive My words
of life for you. Listening is KEY in friendship. I have much to
tell you. I just need an attentive ear more often. Get to the place
where you never make any decisions without consulting me
and asking Me My plan for you. I am into the details... at least
those you include Me in on. My heart is for you, beloved. Trust
me to speak, then do what I say. I lead you into an incredibly
abundant life: abundant mercy and abundant love—like a wild
river overflowing its banks. How about today? Ask Me about
your day today.

### Declarations and Decrees of Truth

I decree and declare that I will EXPECT to hear the voice of my
Father and my Savior, Jesus Christ.
I decree and declare that I will inquire of the Lord for every
decision I make.
I decree and declare that I will bear much fruit in Jesus' name
because He is my vine and I am his branch.
I decree and declare that I will abide in Jesus—daily turning
my thoughts to Him.

# Day 6: Beloved

"For the Holy Spirit makes God's fatherhood real to us as he whispers into our innermost being, "You are God's beloved child!" Romans 8:16 TPT

**Romans 8:15, Isaiah 55:11, Hebrews 4:16, Romans 10:17, Ephesians 2:4-7, Galatians 4:6-7, Hebrews 11:6**

My beloved child, I am fully healing your heart. The truth of who you are is burning away the lies. I did not leave you as an orphan. As my child, you have full access. Not only close proximity to me in my throne room, but also full access in My kingdom. Everything I have is yours. Let this revelation of My love as your Abba Father hit your heart. Climb up on My lap, dear one. My love rushes over you, and it holds you up. All the promises I have spoken over you are coming to fruition. My Word does not return void and faith comes by hearing Me speak my Rhema word. BE LOVED. I call you *beloved*. You've always been loved by Me. You've never had to earn it, and you don't now. You are Mine. You are in my Heavenly family. Rejoice. Rejoice and BE LOVED by Me! I adore you and I've chosen you. Come and sit at our table. Here, intimate fellowship increases. I want you to understand your seat at My table doesn't depend on what you "do." My dear Son has made a way for your total atonement, and He has robed you in His Robe of Righteousness. He has claimed you as part of His faithful bride. I am a rewarder of those who diligently seek Me. Practice My presence. Replace time on your phone with affection and thoughts toward Me. I am waiting on you, My beloved child.

## Declarations and Decrees of Truth

I decree and declare that I am anointed, chosen, and called by the Lord.

I decree and declare that my day will be filled with the wisdom of God.

I decree and declare that I am bold as a lion because Heaven backs me up.

I decree and declare that religion says *DO*, but relationship says *DONE*.

# Day 7: Sacrificial Praise

"After (Paul and Silas) were severely beaten, they were thrown into prison and the jailer was commanded to guard them securely... Paul and Silas, undaunted, prayed in the middle of the night and sang songs of praise to God, while all the other prisoners listened to their worship. Suddenly, a great earthquake shook the foundations of the prison. All at once every prison door flung open and the chains of all the prisoners came loose." Acts 16:23, 25-26 TPT

**Song of Songs 5:16, Nehemiah 8:10, Hebrews 11:1, Romans 4:17, Isaiah 30:21, John 15**

My precious child, I see you. I see every detail of your life. I see your heart to obey Me. I cover you with kisses. There is much gold in you—despite what you are told. Your value comes from Me...your Abba Father, the maker of heaven and earth and keeper of your heart. I come in close to you right now. My love pours over you and causes JOY to bubble up. My joy will be your strength. The world will continue to batter against your boat like a storm on the water. Many do not understand My love. But your joy does not come from your situation, it comes from ME and your extreme value to Me. Begin to **sacrificially praise** Me through every single trial. Worship Me in holiness. Fix your eyes on Me when you are experiencing attack, or swelling emotions from the battering of your boat and I WILL SHIFT THE ATMOSPHERE. I am looking for my sons and daughters to believe Me and trust Me and worship BEFORE the breakthrough. Paul and Silas did this at midnight. In shackles. They chose worship instead of fear. And I turned their worship into breakthrough! My resources are endless for those who step forward in faith, despite what their natural eyes are telling them.

Heavenly realities are the real realities. Speak! Declare! Call into being that which is not yet. Speak my rhema word. Faith comes by hearing and hearing from the words I speak to you. Listen to My Voice of Truth in every moment. Walk with Me... do not turn to the right or to the left—only follow My voice. I will guide you around every obstacle. Those who surrender to Me fully will become pillars in the King's Domain (My Kingdom). Stand firm on My Word and move when My Spirit moves. Do not fear being left behind. I am faithful to the end. My love binds us together in perfect unity. Abide in Me and the fruit will flourish on your vine. People will pick it and eat it and seeds will begin to grow in them as well. Worship and thankfulness are sweet fruits of your trust in Me and My great love for you.

## Declarations and Decrees of Truth

I decree and declare that my God will meet all of my needs, in Jesus' name.

_____

_____

_____

_____

_____

_____

_____

_____

_____

_____

_____

_____

# Day 8: You Represent Jesus to the World

"The One whom God has sent to represent Him will speak the words of God, for God has poured out upon him the FULLNESS of the Holy Spirit with limitation." John 3:34 TPT

Jesus prayed, "I have commissioned them to represent Me, just as you commissioned Me to represent you." John 17:18

**John 7:38, Psalm 40:4, Zephaniah 3:17, James 1:22, 2 Corinthians 10:5**

You are My beloved... and I am yours. I have much to tell you. I see the things ahead, and my weapons are mighty for pulling down strongholds. I sing songs over you that no one can take away. I fill you with my living water so that you may overflow into every life you come upon. Break agreement with the lie that you are not able to do this. As my child, you are a vessel for the light of the gospel. Your feelings are not always the truth. Feelings are fleeting, but the one who stands and walks in the truth—no matter how they are feeling from one day to the next—is obedient and trustworthy. My truth flows from within you and will increase as you study My Word and become it. As I did. Follow Me, My beloved bride. Stepping into risk is pushing past lies of fear and inadequacy. After this step, My anointing upon you flows without measure. My Spirit will teach you what to say and sometimes speak for you. In full surrender, you become the glove, and I am the hand. In this season, there will be more opportunities and more outpouring of My Spirit. You must learn how to walk with my Spirit and flow with Me. As your obedience shines in the smaller assignments, there will be increase.

## Declarations and Decrees of Truth

I decree and declare that I am representing Jesus, in love, everywhere I go.

I decree and declare that lies will be taken captive and will not lead me astray.

I decree and declare that I am a temple of the Holy Spirit, who flows through me in fullness—without measure.

I decree and declare that my worship shifts atmospheres, in Jesus' name.

# Day 9: Let Me Steady Your Heart

"You will keep in perfect peace all who trust in you, all whose thoughts are fixed on you! Trust in the Lord always, for the Lord God is the eternal Rock." Isaiah 26:3-4 NLT

**1 John 4:16,18, Romans 8:38-39, Exodus 14:14, 2 Chronicles 16:9, Psalm 91:1, John 15:4, Isaiah 43:19, Psalm 37:4, Proverbs 3:5-6, Ezekiel 36:26, 2 Corinthians 4:18, 2 Thessalonians 3:3**

Beloved, open your heart more fully to receive from Me. My love manifests in tangible ways. My love toward you is constant—you'll never have to wonder where My love went. I AM LOVE. Nothing can separate you or your family from My love. Not any principality or fear or feeling. My love will conquer all fear that tries to attach to your family. Fear is an illusion. Remember I told you? It's the enemy's main tactic. He is totally defeated and is grasping at everything he can, to make My "sent ones" doubt. Put your confidence in Me. I will fight for you. Praise Me, even in the uncertainty. My hand is steadily upon you. I never lift My hand. Steady your heart in My shadow. My eyes search to and fro, all over the earth for those sold out to Me who need My strength. The walk I call you to is impossible— on your own. You must intertwine yourself into the vine: Jesus. My grace empowers you to walk out what truth calls you to. I AM sufficient for you. In this season, I am doing MANY new things. I am birthing something new in your life. You will not always be stuck in the waiting. Delight yourself in Me, child, and I will give you the desires of your heart that I placed there. My plans are great. I am developing extreme trust in Me within your heart. I need your total and absolute trust. Begin to trust Me and what I say OVER what you see with your eyes. Rejoice this day. I have put a new heart of flesh in you and you are Mine. Set your heart on things above, not earthly things, for the things of earth will fade, but My kingdom lasts forever.

## Declarations and Decrees of Truth

I decree and declare that I am safe and secure in my Father's hand.
I decree and declare that the Lord's peace covers my heart today.
I decree and declare that God's love conquers all my fears.

# DAY 10: STAND ON MY PROMISES

"Therefore, put on every piece of God's armor so you
will be able to resist the enemy in the time of evil.
Then after the battle you will still be standing firm."
Ephesians 6:13 NLT

**2 Thessalonians 3:3, Romans 4:17, Proverbs 18:21,
Job 22:27-28, 2 Samuel 22:31, Genesis 1:27,
1 Corinthians 6:19, Isaiah 60:1-5, Isaiah 54:10**

My child, nothing takes Me by surprise. Stand on My Word
and My promises, beloved. Abraham believed me—even when
his body was too old to father a child physically. The physical realm is only part of the equation. The spiritual realm, or
unseen realm, is what you speak into when you "call into being
that which is not yet" (Romans 4:17). You speak My truth in the
spiritual realm—and the power of your words IN MY NAME
causes things in the natural realm to line up with the will of
your Father. Take dominion in my authority. Stand. You are
seated with Christ in heavenly places as a child of the MOST
HIGH. Speak life to this situation and watch your words of
truth come to fruition in My timing. You were made in My
image; in the image of God we created you. Shake off the lies
that you are a victim. You are a mighty warrior. My blood flows
through your veins. The Holy Spirit dwells in you like the Holy
of Holies. Rise up. Speak out my promises! You are Mine.

## Declarations and Decrees of Truth

I decree and declare that I believe God's Word over what I see
with my eyes.
I decree and declare that I will fix my eyes on Jesus, especially
when the battle for my mind and thoughts is raging.
I decree and declare that I am a mighty warrior for the
kingdom of God.
I decree and declare that I am no victim; I am a victorious
child of God.

# DAY 11: CONNECT WITH MY HEART

"How deeply intimate and far reaching is his love!
How enduring and inclusive it is! Endless love beyond
measurement that transcends our understanding—
this extravagant love pours into you until you are
filled to overflowing with the fullness of God!"
Ephesians 3:19 TPT

**Isaiah 42:13-16, 1 Corinthians 2:9-10, Matthew 11:12,
John 7:38, Psalm 118:24, Ephesians 1:17, 1 John 2:24,
Genesis 3:1-7, Psalm 37:3-4**

Beloved, our intimacy is worth rising early. Relationships are the point at which hearts connect. I love to reach down and connect with your heart. I love to share My thoughts with you and teach you about My kingdom. The kingdom of God is coming violently upon the earth through love. In this season, truth and love will be abundant—as will My wonders. I will no longer stay silent. My Spirit will flow freely—like a mighty rushing river—through My sons and daughters, to the world. The sons and daughters who give Me their whole hearts and lives will undergo incredible transformation. They will never be the same. This is the day I have made... rejoice and put all your hopes in Me. I am your Father and I want the very best for you. Negative thoughts and doubts are from the one who wants to separate you from My will. But he is defeated. His power is an illusion. He only has the amount of power and persuasion you give him. Do not come into agreement with the lies he speaks over you. He dangles things before your eyes and says, "Did God really say...?" Isn't that what he said to Eve as well? His games haven't changed much. But as for Me, My ways are perfect. My plans are to prosper you in your journey with Me. My constant pursuit of you shows My heart's desire to be in close fellowship with my family. Come to the table. You have a special place beside Me.

## Declarations and Decrees of Truth

I decree and declare that my time with the Lord will be fiercely guarded every day.

I decree and declare that my life belongs to the Living God...
Jesus, I surrender all.
I decree and declare that I will not fall into agreement with lies
from the enemy but will align myself with God's truth.

_____

_____

_____

_____

_____

_____

_____

_____

_____

_____

_____

_____

_____

_____

_____

_____

_____

# Day 12: You Are My Delight

"For now is the time to arise and come away with me…
Let me see your radiant face and hear your sweet voice.
How beautiful your eyes of worship and your lovely
voice in prayer." Song of Songs 2:13b-14 TPT

**Isaiah 50:4, Song of Songs 6:4 TPT, Psalm 16:7, 1 Thessalonians 5:17, Ephesians 6:17, Psalm 91:15, Philippians 4:6-7, 1 John 2:8**

Beloved child, My heart delights in you. I love to come near you and overshadow you with My presence in the night watches. I always draw near when we meet in the secret place. You have no idea how radiantly My love shines for you. Today, as you move through your day of activities, bring your affection back to Me every few minutes. Put your phone down. Give My Spirit space in your day and do not forsake intercession. I believe you are starting to understand how praying directly relates to breakthroughs. Pray in the Spirit more often. My Spirit knows exactly what to pray for all situations.

Do not give up! Stand in faith. I honor those who stand with their eyes fixed on Me and My words. I look to and fro throughout the whole earth to find My beloveds with FAITH to STAND despite the storm. My Spirit strengthens those willing to endure. When worry or fearful thoughts come, speak out My provision for that thought. This way fear is crushed, and you declare your partnership with the truth… with thanksgiving. You are Mine and My kingdom is being made manifest through you.

## Declarations and Decrees of Truth

I decree and declare that I was created for constant fellowship with my Father.
I decree and declare that I am no longer a slave to fear, I am a child of God.
I decree and declare that I will stand on the promises of God and I will see victory.
I decree and declare that today I fix my eyes on you Jesus—for You hold my heart.

# Day 13: Our Intimacy First

"I pray that the Father of glory, the God of our Lord Jesus Christ, would impart to you the riches of the Spirit of wisdom and the Spirit of revelation to know him through your deepening intimacy with him." Ephesians 1:17 TPT

**James 5:7, Isaiah 43:18-19, 2 Corinthians 13:14, Hebrews 12:2, Isaiah 58:8, Deuteronomy 31:6, John 14:6, Ephesians 6:10, Romans 4:17, Luke 10:40-42, Ephesians 5:1**

My beloved child, I come close. My presence will encapsulate you, and I surround you with My love. I am about to rain down on you. The latter rain is at hand. My rain is an outpouring of My Spirit in such a way that mankind has not seen yet. This is why My Word says, "Behold, I am doing a new thing!" Streams will flow in the desert and, in dry and arid hearts, there will spring up a drenching water that revitalizes and causes new life to spring forth, bearing much fruit. YOU are living in these days. Beloved… our intimacy must remain first. Do not take your eyes off of Me. Pride and self-absorption are always alluring, but those who stay in full communion and FIX their eyes on Me will renew their strength and will be raised up to model My love and My call to intimacy with their Father.

My hands are upon you mightily... I go before you and I am your rear guard. Though others fall away in fear, you will be strong and courageous when you have your eyes fixed on Me. Walking on water will become a thing we do together every day. Trust Me with everything. I will sustain you in every situation. You will continue to declare and decree My promises over every wall, dead-end, and mountain that you face. You will speak truth and stand. Things will move out of your way as you walk near — because of your faith in MY WORDS, rather than what the enemy tries to detour you with, in the natural. This is why I say: "FIX YOUR EYES ON ME." Look into My eyes, beloved. I am the WAY, the TRUTH, and the LIFE. All creation knows My name. I know the way. Listen for My direction. My guidance. My love. I continually speak these over you. You are My sent one. I have set you apart. Cling to Me like Mary did. As you do, the gospel will be demonstrated as you become a conduit of My love in every situation. You are Mine.

## Declarations and Decrees of Truth

I decree and declare that I will look to Jesus in full communion for deepening intimacy.

I decree and declare that the light of Jesus shines through me.

_____

_____

_____

_____

_____

_____

_____

_____

_____

_____

_____

_____

_____

_____

_____

# Day 14: Stand and Trust in Me

"Trust in the Lord with all your heart; do not depend on your own understanding. Seek His will in all you do, and he will show you which path to take." Proverbs 3:5-6 NLT

**Ephesians 6:13-14, Hebrews 12:2, Romans 6:18, Hosea 2:19, Ephesians 4:24, Job 22:28 NASB, Matthew 11:28**

My righteousness drenches you with purity. My Holiness reflects off of you as you fix your eyes on Me and imitate and walk with Me, in love, into hopeless situations. By My hand, you will have what you need. The hope of the gospel reflects My revelation light from your eyes. Lay your life down. Give it fully over to Me. In that place is full dependence on My path for you. Lay down your desire to control. Trust in Me. The only one you can change is yourself.

So, my beloved one... love. Love does not keep a record of wrongs. Love rejoices in the truth. Can you rejoice on this side of a breakthrough? When you stand and contend for needed breakthroughs, you prove your trust in Me. Words are cheap, but actions prove what is in your heart. Decree and declare My truths over your family and over the difficult circumstances. The more disheartening or frustrating the situation, the greater opportunity for Me to show Myself strong on your behalf. I am faithful to My sons and daughters. You must learn to speak the truth and stand. Focus on My love and past provision in the hard moments. Begin to recall and thank Me for past breakthroughs and answered prayers. In no time, you will shift the atmosphere to a faith-filled atmosphere of testimony and remembrance. Proclaim My faithfulness to DO IT AGAIN. Declare My promises; declare them with confidence. Do not worry about the mountain looming over you. I specialize in moving these for My beloved children. Just as I sent you across the world for the one, I would stop at nothing to make a way for your breakthrough in My providential timing. Just trust Me, My child. Rest in My loving arms that are embracing you right now. I am enough for you.

## Declarations and Decrees of Truth

I decree and declare that no worry can find a place to land in my heart. These burdens are yours, Lord.

I decree and declare that I lay down my control of situations and people and give You the reins, oh God.

_____

_____

_____

_____

_____

_____

_____

_____

_____

_____

_____

_____

_____

_____

_____

_____

# Day 15: I AM Your Burden Bearer

"Praise be to the Lord, to God our Savior, who
daily bears our burdens." Psalm 68:19 NIV

**Psalm 104:4 TPT, John 6:48, Exodus 3:14, John 8:12, Matthew 7:24,
John 7:38, Songs of Songs 4:15 TPT, Luke 10:19, Hebrews 1-2,
Matthew 6:22 KJV, Ephesians 5:1, Revelation 22:17**

My child, hold your hands up and give Me everything. Let Me breathe on all the burdens and worries, then you will be free. Stay in this place of committing all the things you're dealing with to Me and I will give you peace of mind in exchange. My ministers are a flame of fire and must fully trust in Me: I AM.

I AM your bread of life.

I AM your Living Water.

I AM the light of the world, and I shine brightly into your heart.

I AM the Rock of all ages—a firm place for you to stand.

I AM an all-consuming fire, and unworthy things in your life burn up in my presence.

Although the battle rages, we are victorious. Call into being a hunger and desire for holiness and purity—a breaking of the stronghold of compromise. You are a strong plant with extensive roots. I water your roots with My living water from the secret place of your innermost being. This is why you never run dry. Everything you need comes from Me: your source.

You are not on the defense. The kingdom reigns. You have authority, but you must keep your eyes on Me and remember who you are. When the enemy's words in your mind or when others try to stifle you, throw off those words and laugh. YOU ARE MINE. Do not let his insults and mockery slow your momentum down. Come back to Me in your thoughts and I will remind you how close I AM. He has no power over you as you walk with Me in holiness and righteousness. So, throw off the sin that so easily entangles and FIX your eyes on Me— as I continue to perfect your faith, beloved. Instead of sadness, respond to that opposition with My love and mercy. This will defeat the enemy, and he will be cut off. I see your heart and your eye that is single—singly focused on me. I strengthen you today. Go in My love and power to overcome all the schemes of the enemy. Be imitators of God and walk in love.

## Declarations and Decrees of Truth

I decree and declare that I will turn away from anxiety and express thanksgiving to God.

_____

_____

_____

_____

_____

_____

_____

_____

_____

_____

_____

_____

_____

_____

_____

_____

# DAY 16: SPEAK LIFE

"My wonderful God, you are to be praised above all;
teach me the power of your decrees! I speak continually of your laws as I recite out loud your counsel to me."
Psalms 119:12-13 TPT

**2 Corinthians 2:14, Proverbs 18:21, 2 Peter 1:3-4,
Ephesians 1, Exodus 33:11, Psalm 91**

My child, I lead you in a triumphant procession because the victory has been won. The enemy of your soul is defeated — but he won't go down without a fight. He picks that fight with My people and leads the lost deeper into captivity. But the light of My gospel shines. I am faithful to rescue and breathe life into those who feel lifeless — stuck in the illusion that they are nothing. Nothing could be further from the truth. My blood flows through your veins. You are partakers of the divine nature, beloved. The enemy is beside himself over it. He wants to tell you things to keep you in captivity, so you can not affect My kingdom because you are trapped in his lies. Speak out those thoughts and cast them down. Speak out the opposite and partner with what I am saying about you. Your value to me is intensely great and no one else could do what I have created you to do. You can affect certain people that others cannot. My love completely surrounds you. I can't wait to share all that I have planned for your life. As we move toward full communion, I will show you more and more of who I AM... as I did with Moses.

## Declarations and Decrees of Truth

I decree and declare that I am the head and not the tail. My God is turning things around in my life.
I decree and declare a restoration of all that has been lost and stolen from my family.
I decree and declare that I am coming into the new. I decree a renewing of all things in my life.
I decree and declare that I will follow Jesus in triumph because I am a part of His bride.

# Day 17: Stand in My Love

"Be on your guard; stand firm in the faith; be courageous; be strong. **Let all that you do be done in love.**"
1 Corinthians 16:13-14 NASB

**Ephesians 1:3, John 16:33, Revelation 12:11, John 10:27, 1 Corinthians 13:4-8, Isaiah 55:11, Romans 4:17, 2 Timothy 1:7, Jeremiah 31:3, 1 Peter 5:8, Isaiah 40:8, Ephesians 6:13**

My heart has unending devotion for my "sent ones." You've been called out—chosen, selected by Me to do mighty exploits. My peace I give you: In this world, there will be trouble, but be encouraged, I have overcome the world. And you are also an overcomer. I am pleased with you, beloved. Do not listen to the voice that seeks to bring you down low, to destruction. My sheep will listen to My voice. I know them, and they follow Me. So follow Me. Move when I move, do what I do. I am faithful to speak to you, My child. My love is constant—pouring over you. And My love never fails. As you receive it, give it away freely. You were created to be a conduit of My overwhelming love. There is no chain this love can't break. My plans are good.

Every word of my Word is true. It will never return void. I AM the Lord of Hosts and I AM your Defender. I am teaching you how to stand firm with My Word. Call into being that which is not. Call into being freedom for that one bound in your life. Come against fear and intimidation, because that is not your portion. Rest and abide in Me today. I am filling you with My strength and My peace. I AM. Keep your eyes on what I am doing, not what the enemy is trying to accomplish through lies and illusion. Stand firm, speaking out My promises in scripture. STAND. STAND. You are Mine and you are extremely valuable to My heart. My love is everlasting.

## Declarations and Decrees of Truth

I decree and declare that my God will meet all my needs, in the mighty name of Jesus.

I decree and declare that the love of Jesus will flow through me to others as I surrender myself to be a conduit of divine love.

I decree and declare that I will see freedom from lies believed by my family, in the name of Jesus Christ.

# DAY 18: I WILL RESCUE YOU

"Even to your old age and gray hairs I am he, I am he who will sustain you. I have made you and I will carry you; I will sustain you and I will rescue you." Isaiah 46:4 NIV

**Psalm 57:1, Isaiah 40:31, James 1:17, Psalm 91:15-16, Song of Songs 2:4**

Beloved, I have you protected under My wing. Rest in My shadow. Those that wait upon the Lord will renew their strength. They will mount up on wings like eagles and soar ABOVE the natural circumstances. Hold tightly to My promises. My Word is truth and it does not fall to the ground. Even to your gray hair I sustain you. I will sustain you, carry you, and rescue you and your family. There is a rainbow over your home. I will deliver My promises fully to you. Find your peace in Me. I am your Father—who never changes, as does the shifting sand. I am the one who gazes at you. My hand is firmly upon your life. No evil will prevail... he is a defeated foe. You've been attacked because of our intimacy because you have learned to hear Me directly. This threatens your adversary, but his efforts are futile. You stand in MY victory. I will rescue you and show you My salvation. Rest in me… do not worry or fear. I breathe My peace over you today. My banner over you is love, joy, and peace. Step into these today.

## Declarations and Decrees of Truth

I decree and declare that my peace is from the Lord, not my circumstances.
I decree and declare that the enemy is a defeated foe and I am victorious because I am in Christ Jesus.
I decree and declare that I abide in the shadow of the Almighty where I am safe.
I decree and declare that my fear is crushed in His presence and by His perfect love.

# Day 19: I Gave
## Everything for YOU

"...Now we have been stamped with the seal of the promised Holy Spirit. He is given to us like an engagement ring is given to a bride, as the first installment of what's coming! He is our hope-promise of a future inheritance which seals us until we have all of redemption's promises and experience complete freedom — all for the supreme glory and honor of God!" Ephesians 1:13-14 TPT

**Matthew 5:9, Matthew 10:11-14, 2 Corinthians 3:18, Psalm 61:5, Matthew 17:20, John 10:10, Psalm 23, 1 John 4:15-16, 18, James 4:7**

Blessed are the peacemakers for they will inherit the kingdom of God. You are a releaser of My Spirit's peace. You bring My presence into every establishment you visit. Understand that you can release this aspect of My kingdom because you have full access with your inheritance. You are a beloved child. You are always welcome and always family... never an outsider. I paid a high price for you and I to have intimate fellowship. I'm still teaching you about the full reality of who you are. Never take your sonship for granted. Hold tight to My Word. When spoken in My authority, My Word shifts things and moves mountains. Turn toward Me, seek Me and My kingdom in every moment and My Spirit will draw you into deeper intimacy. I have heard your heart cry, but it begins with you, my love. My heart is fully connected to you.

The enemy seeks to steal, kill, and destroy the lives of My beloveds with his lies and illusions. But I have given My life for their victory. The battle has been won. If you come into agreement with something, it is empowered in your life. So, you are giving that thing permission to rule over you. Agree with ME. I gave everything to give you everything. My faithful promises do not return void. I am with you. My love never fails. Even when you walk through the valley of the shadow of death — you will fear no evil. I prepare a table for you to sit with Me even in the presence of the enemy. I will hold onto you and comfort you. My perfect love and faithfulness drive away every fear. Praise and thankfulness shift atmospheres and cause the enemy to flee from you.

## Declarations and Decrees of Truth

I decree and declare that I am in agreement with what the Father says about me.

I decree and declare that I can release peace into situations because the Prince of Peace lives in me.

_____

_____

_____

_____

_____

_____

_____

_____

_____

_____

_____

_____

_____

_____

_____

# Day 20: I Am Your Friend and Provider

"This is why the scriptures say: Things never discovered or heard of before, things beyond our ability to imagine— these are the many things God has in store for all his lovers. But now God unveils these profound realities to us by the Spirit. Yes, he has revealed to us *his inmost heart* and deepest mysteries through the Holy Spirit, who constantly explores all things." 1 Corinthians 2:9,10 TPT

**2 Timothy 1:7, Isaiah 55:11, 2 Corinthians 5:20, Psalm 81:10, John 6:63, James 1:5-8, Matthew 7:7-8, Malachi 3:10**

Beloved, you are beautiful to me. When I gave My life for you and rose from the dead, My goodness, power, and love were on display. My spoken and written Word will not return to Me without accomplishing all I sent them to do. My words become Spirit and life. My love for you is lavish, you would not be able to handle it in full measure. So I give you glimpses. You are so precious in My sight. You are My ambassador, My mouthpiece. Open your mouth and I will fill it with truth. Connect yourself to Me and I will lead you in the way that you should go.

My love for you is wild in pursuit. I am constantly pursuing you and inviting you into deeper levels of intimacy. Our intimate fellowship can be constant and consistent, once you train yourself to bring your thoughts back to Me. I want to share My innermost thoughts with you, as a friend would. I am looking for those who will commit to do the same. My wisdom provision is available to you as you ask and seek Me. All good and perfect wisdom comes from Me, and I make it available to you. But I do not force it on My people. Those who seek—find, and the door will be opened unto them. My hand personally opens doors and ushers you into new seasons and new places. But I need full surrender, willing sacrifice, and full trust. Trust Me, My precious child. My storehouse is full of blessings for those who are willing to trust Me in RISK and SACRIFICE. My provision overflows.

## Declarations and Decrees of Truth

I decree and declare that God will reveal Himself to me in ways abundantly above what I can ask or even think.

I decree and declare that I am filled with the Lord's joy, peace, and hope, by the power of the Holy Spirit.

I decree and declare that I will be led by the Holy Spirit in every direction that I walk.

_____

_____

_____

_____

_____

_____

_____

_____

_____

_____

_____

_____

_____

_____

_____

_____

# Day 21: My Love Will Sustain You

"I am the sprouting vine and you're my branches. As you live in union with me as your source, fruitfulness will stream from within you — but when you live separated from me you are powerless… But if you live in life-union with me and if my words live powerfully within you — then you can ask whatever you desire and it will be done." John 15:5, 7 TPT

**2 Peter 1:4, 2 Timothy 2:12, Ephesians 5:1-2, John 7:38, Matthew 5:10-12, Matthew 11:28-30 TPT, Psalm 68:19, Colossians 3:12-17**

Blessed is the one who chooses Me above all else. They will walk with Me in the heavenly realms in one accord with My heart. They will not grow weary and give up — even amidst severe trial. I constantly pour life, strength, and supernatural peace into those who are actively walking with Me. Those who are attached to the vine will reap the benefits and much fruit My Father has given Me. You are partakers of My divine nature. My power flows through your life. When people look at you, they see Me and My love. My love overflows from those who constantly give it away. The more you release and give out, the more you are given. This is why I said there would be rivers of living water. A river constantly flows... and so it is with My love. My love is patient. In your full surrender to My ways, you will have patience to deal with your difficulties. When people come in opposition towards you, I am with you. In the same way, I was mocked and called names and My Father poured his love into Me as well. I hold onto you extra tight in those moments. Turn your thoughts and affections to Me and I will give you the words to speak. When you feel anger rise up, release it to Me, for it is I they persecute. You must forgive every time. This keeps your heart pure. I will sustain you until the breakthrough comes. Focus on Me and My purposes for your day. I will carry your burdens. Declare and decree what I've said and enter into praise and thanksgiving in faith for what is about to happen.

## Declarations and Decrees of Truth

I decree and declare that I truly am the object of His deepest love and affection.

I decree and declare that Jesus fills with me grace to endure and discouragement flees from me.

_____

_____

_____

_____

_____

_____

_____

_____

_____

_____

_____

_____

_____

_____

_____

_____

_____

# Day 22: I Am Your Protector

"His massive arms are wrapped around you, protecting
you. You can run under his covering of majesty and
hide. His arms of faithfulness are a shield keeping you
from harm...For here is what the Lord has spoken to me:
"Because you have delighted in me as my great lover, I
will greatly protect you. I will set you in a high place,
safe and secure before my face." Psalms 91:4, 14 TPT

**Deuteronomy 31:6, Ephesians 6:10-13, 2 Timothy 2:19 NLT,
1 Peter 5:10, John 10:27-29, 1 Peter 1:5-6**

Beloved, you are not alone—despite what your feelings tell
you. My love for you crashes over you. I completely surround
you in protection from the enemy. I have sent more than one of
My messengers to wrap you in protection from demonic enti-
ties, which seek to destroy. Stand strong in Me and My mighty
power! Do not forget who I've created you to be… a mighty
warrior! Stand firm on My truth; it is a firm foundation—a rock
for you to stand on. Praise Me in the storm. Praise Me, despite
the soaking rain and even in the lightning. I am your shelter
and your protector. Thank Me for the rescue before it comes.
Trust Me. Trust Me, My child. I am faithful to my beloveds.
Nothing can take you out of My grasp in your surrender. My
love for you ran red (on the cross). Real love came down to
break every chain. Never underestimate the power of the cross.
I paid it all for FULL VICTORY. It is finished. Freedom is paid
in full. And I am yours.

## Declarations and Decrees of Truth

I decree and declare that Jesus is holding onto me, no matter
what my feelings seem to be.
I decree and declare that I will see these chains broken by the
blood of the Lamb.
I decree and declare that I will speak and declare truth over
myself and my family today.

# DAY 23: I DRAW NEAR TO YOU TODAY

"Therefore, submit to God. Resist the devil and he will flee from you. Draw near to God and He will draw near to you."
James 4:7-8 NKJV

**Jeremiah 29:11, John 10:10, Ephesians 6:10-13,
Matthew 11:28-30, 2 Corinthians 10:4-6, James 1:12,
John 15:4 NKJV, Galatians 5.26, Psalm 18:18,19**

My beloved one, I have good plans for your life. Plans of fruitful abundance and freedom from chains that hold you. This season was one to draw a line in the sand and to draw you into My loving arms. You do not need to find your value in what you do, it's found in who you are and who you belong to. I want you to lay all well-meaning distractions down—so that you have one focus: Me. You haven't seen anything yet. Put on all the armor I have provided for you. This is a war. But I am teaching you how to claim the victory that has been WON for you. DO NOT FEAR, focus on Me. Come to Me and give Me every burden. Let Me take them for you. My yoke is easy and My burden is light. As you do, you will find rest for your soul. I hear the lies that come through your mind. Reject them and throw them under your feet. Do not compare yourself to others. You must make a decision… what is it you are really after? Comparison leads to jealousy and coveting. When these thoughts come, reject them and worship. Worship Me in the splendor of holiness. I am with you and I am faithful. Blessed is the one who perseveres under trial, because great is your reward. Press into My presence today. I am drawing near to you, beloved. Trust in Me. I know the way through the wilderness to a spacious place, where the lilies grow. Abide in Me today.

## Declarations and Decrees of Truth

I decree and declare that I am free of fear because I am covered by the love of the Father.
I decree and declare that as I speak out thankfulness and praise the enemy will flee.
I decree and declare that the Voice of Truth will lead me in the way I should go.

# Day 24: Look into My Eyes

"For you reach into my heart. With one flash of your eyes I am undone by your love, my beloved, my equal, my bride. You leave me breathless— I am overcome by merely a glance from your worshiping eyes, for you have stolen my heart. I am held hostage by your love and by the graces of righteousness shining upon you." Song of Songs 4:9 TPT

**Mark 2:22, Hebrews 12:2, John 10:27, Deuteronomy 31:8 NLT, Matthew 6:6, Matthew 11:28, Hebrews 1:3, Galatians 5:22-23 TPT, Isaiah 46:4, Matthew 6:26-27, 2 Timothy 1:7**

Don't be afraid of change, beloved. Give Me the old, dry, cracked wineskin. I am doing something new. The new wineskin I have for you has much more capacity because the coming outpouring of my Spirit is mighty to save and mighty to display my wonders. Things will look different. Fix your eyes and ears on Me and I will show you. The unknown is only scary if you go alone. You are not alone because I lead you. I can see the destination of your destiny. Trust me, beloved. Come away with me to our secret place. Let go of all these burdens and give them to Me. Hold My hand and look into My eyes. My love sustains your soul and I speak My love to your heart. You know you're seated with Me at My heavenly table. My love is limitless. Hold fast to Me… and fall back into My arms in full trust. Am I big enough to catch you? Now that you know who I am, would I let you fall to the ground? Not even a sparrow falls to the ground without My notice. I have wild dreams for you and have given you My Spirit of love, power, wisdom, and revelation to step into the plans I have for you for success.

## Declarations and Decrees of Truth

I decree and declare that I trust in the Lord with my life; I will not be afraid.
I decree and declare that Jesus is mighty to save, and He will display His wonders through me.
I decree and declare that I am my Beloved's and He is mine… I am the bride of CHRIST.

# Day 25: I Am Your Source

"What delight comes to the one who follows God's ways!
He won't walk in step with the wicked, nor share the sin-
ner's way, nor be found sitting in the scorner's seat. His
pleasure and passion are remaining true to the Word of
"I Am," meditating day and night in the true revelation
of light. He will be standing firm like a flourishing tree
planted by God's design, deeply rooted by the brooks
of bliss, bearing fruit in every season of his life. He is
never dry, never fainting, ever blessed, ever prosperous."
Psalms 1:1-3 TPT

**Ephesians 6:17-18, Revelation 3:10, Romans 5:1-5,
2 Peter 1:2-8, Luke 13:18-19, 1 Peter 1:3-9**

Beloved, believe Me and My Word. Speak truth over your
situations and there will be a shift. Perseverance is the key.
Perseverance says you believe Me, My Word and My promises over the reality you behold with your eyes. This is another
reason to stay plugged into your source. I am your source of
life, love, grace, mercy, joy, deliverance, and provision. I am
the healer. You are My amazing vessel that My love and power
flows through to bring miracles into people's paradigms. Your
faith began as a mustard seed—but now it's growing into the
biggest tree in the garden. It has its roots watered from under-
ground because it's planted by streams of water. LIVING
WATER. When the drought comes and the sun scorches its
leaves, the tree is inwardly flourishing because its roots get
water from the flowing river—not the sources that are typ-
ical or expected. This is how it is with you, My beloved one.
Not only am I giving you living water every day, but a living
HOPE to stand on my promises for you and every member of
your family. This supernatural stamina only comes to those
who fully trust Me and live their lives in faithful obedience to
what I say.

### Declarations and Decrees of Truth

I decree and declare that I will stand on the TRUTH of the
Word until my experience lines up with it.

I decree and declare that My God is my source of life and godliness.
I decree and declare that I am a child of the King and in my surrender, God flows miracles through my life.

_____

_____

_____

_____

_____

_____

_____

_____

_____

_____

_____

_____

_____

_____

_____

_____

_____

# Day 26: I Pull You in Close to Me, Beloved

"Let the morning bring me word of your unfailing love,
for I have put my trust in you. Show me the way I
should go, for to you I entrust my life." Psalm 143:8 NIV

**James 4:8, 2 Chronicles 16:9, Galatians 4:7, John 15:15,
Jude 1:21, Lamentations 3:22, Psalm 91:1**

Beloved one, I love you and I simply cannot wait for you to awaken each morning. I always notice when I am the first thought on your mind. Come to Me for intimate friendship. Tell Me your innermost thoughts. Bring Me everything. Our communion is as deep and as often as you draw near. I am always waiting on you to turn toward Me with your love. My eyes search to and fro, looking for those whose hearts are fully turned towards Me. They will reap great rewards. My love has been poured out. I wait for my lovers to come and take it and reciprocate my love. Then, out of this place of intimate love and friendship, they serve Me in the kingdom. It's a totally different dynamic rather than servants and workers admiring Me from afar. Serving Me apart from intimate relationship causes burnout. They will never fully understand their identity as sons and daughters... or My love. But this is not with you. I see your beautiful, faithful heart, reaching for Me. I pull you in, my beloved. I pull you in close... in the shadow.

## Declarations and Decrees of Truth

I decree and declare that, as a child of God, I receive the Father's Love until I overflow.
I decree and declare that today I will love those in my path with the overflowing love I have been given.
I decree and declare that I am protected and sustained by my Father in every situation.

# Day 27: Intimacy Is What I Desire

"Cease *striving* and know that I am God; I will be exalted
among the nations; I will be exalted in the earth."
Psalm 46:10 NASB

**Proverbs 22:11, Ephesians 1:3-14, Galatians 4:4-7,
1 John 4:15-17, John 17:3, 1 Corinthians 3:11-15,
Matthew 5:8, Psalm 32:11, 2 Timothy 2:21**

My child, there is a great deal of striving, and many
churches are teaching My people they must "work" to know
me. An intimate relationship with Me isn't based on what you
do to *earn* My love. Intimacy is your inheritance as sons and
daughters. It's who you are, because of what I sacrificed. Your
salvation was free, but once you are born again, you are a part
of My royal family. You are mine. As a child loves their father
and wants to spend time with him just because of their love,
so it should be in My kingdom. Many of My children in My
churches are being taught to work and strive, AND THEN I
will do things for them as a result of their obedience. I am not
a slave-driver. I am the ultimate Father of love. Works done, to
get close to Me, are driven by wrong motives. I have already
paid the wages. Come to me in humility and repentance with
pure motives and an unadulterated desire to KNOW ME, and
a willingness for Me to fully know YOU. Full surrender. Don't
bring Me what you do to earn my love. Those things are like
wood, hay, and stubble, and will be burned up in my refining
fire. Bring Me your pure heart with no agenda. Come to Me,
and I will reveal myself to you. I will show you My glory
and My love.

## Declarations and Decrees of Truth

I decree and declare that I am who He says I am: a child of God,
one in spirit with Him.
I decree and declare that Christ lives in me, and I am a partaker
in His divine nature.
I decree and declare that the veil has been torn, inviting me in,
to the presence of the living God.

# DAY 28: WALK IN LOVE

"Be imitators of God in everything you do, for then you will represent your Father as his beloved sons and daughters. And continue to walk surrendered to the extravagant love of Christ, for he surrendered his life as a sacrifice for us. His great love for us was pleasing to God, like an aroma of adoration—a sweet healing fragrance." Ephesians 5:1-2 TPT

**Psalm 138:2, Revelation 3:12, James 3:17, Matthew 7:24, 2 Corinthians 12:19, Isaiah 40:8, Psalm 91:1-2**

Beloved, My love reaches beyond the limits of your mind. I exalt My Word above My own name. Let My Word wash over your mind and heart. The truth of the gospel cuts away all lies the enemy has attached. It is pure and peaceable, and every good gift comes out of this place. I have many things to tell you, child. Every prayer and heart cry have been heard. Walk with me today... open your ears and your eyes to My perspective. Let me show you My ways. Those who choose to obey Me and My words are like a wise man who builds his house on the rock. The waves cannot reach him or toss him because his feet are firmly planted in Me. Those who do not love their life more than they love Me will be pillars in My house. These are the ones that I can trust—those who obey Me at any cost, no matter how they appear. My grace is sufficient for you, beloved. My strength is magnified in your weakness. The flowers will fade and the grass will wither, but those who hope in Me will renew their strength from glory to glory. Nothing will be impossible for you. I will give you the grace to walk out what truth calls you to: living in truth, honor, love, and compassion. These are the virtues My children exhibit as they walk in My shadow. Follow Me and be imitators of God, as you walk in love.

## Declarations and Decrees of Truth

I decree and declare that I am anointed for the assignment and calling put on my life.

I decree and declare that I can decree a thing and it shall be established.

I decree and declare that I am appointed by heaven to change the world with the love of Jesus.

# DAY 29: I WILL FIGHT FOR YOU

"...This is what the Lord says: Do not be afraid! **Don't be discouraged by this mighty army, for the battle is not yours, but God's**. Tomorrow, march out against them. You will find them coming up through the ascent of Ziz at the end of the valley that opens into the wilderness of Jeruel. But you will not even need to fight. Take your positions; then stand still and watch the Lord's victory. He is with you, O people of Judah and Jerusalem. Do not be afraid or discouraged. Go out against them tomorrow, for the Lord is with you!"
2 Chronicles 20:15-17 NLT

Exodus 14:14, Ephesians 1:11-14, Matthew 17:20, 2 Chronicles 20:1-30, Isaiah 14:27, Isaiah 45:11-12, James 4:7, Deuteronomy 20:4, Proverbs 18:21, Romans 4:17-21, Hebrews 11:1

I move the mountains through your lips. Believe you are who I say you are. My Word is true; you can stand on it. King Jehoshaphat sought Me with all his heart. He believed I would intervene. He trusted Me, and in the trust... He worshiped. Worship in the face of war shows your trust. Crush fear by focusing your gaze on me: the One who demolishes your enemies with a word. Who can stop Me? Who has anything on the creator of all things? I formed the stars and told the planets where to stand. In a breath, I created everything that is. I am still *I AM*. You submit to Me and the enemy will flee. Declare My victory over your situation. This battle is Mine. Your job is to declare, believe, and expect that I will deliver. As My child, you are an heir. All I have is yours. But most of My children don't understand their inheritance. They do not understand what's already theirs... or what could be theirs by the power I have put in your words. Call into being that which is not. Continue to declare your freedom over the situation. You just don't know who you are, beloved. Speak in faith that I am fighting your battles. Believe Me and My Word over your circumstances. This is faith. Go worship Me and declare your freedom.

## Declarations and Decrees of Truth

I decree and declare that I will worship in full trust like King Jehoshaphat.

I decree and declare that all my battles today belong to the Lord; He will fight for me.

I decree and declare that the Lord has not given me a spirit of fear, but a spirit of POWER, LOVE, and a SOUND MIND.

_____

_____

_____

_____

_____

_____

_____

_____

_____

_____

_____

_____

_____

_____

_____

_____

# Day 30: Follow Me and Stay Close

"God, for whom and through whom everything was made,
chose to bring many children into glory. And it was only
right that he should make Jesus, through his suffering,
a perfect leader, fit to bring them into their salvation."
Hebrews 2:10 NLT

**Genesis 6:9, Mark 8:34, Matthew 9:37-38, Acts 12:6-11, Proverbs 16:3,
Deuteronomy 33:27, Matthew 14:28, Psalm 119:89-91, Ephesians 1:17-18**

Beloved, you are a trailblazer. Staying close to Me, in intimate fellowship, is the key for leading others. Imitate My Son and they will not be led astray. He was sent to lead My sons and daughters to glory through a life sacrificed. Laying down your will for Mine reaps great reward. There is a harvesting of many souls coming that is so great, it will be like nothing you have ever seen or imagined. My child, hold the hand of My Spirit, there is a wild ride ahead—an adventure! My angelic messengers go with you everywhere you go, protecting you from the schemes plotted against you and My plans for you. Submit your plans to Me and you will succeed. My everlasting arms keep you in balance as you commune with Me. Do not forsake coming into My presence. This will become absolutely pertinent every day as you begin to walk on the water with My Son. Devour My Word daily as this brings you solid foundation to your life and what I am calling you to do. My Spirit will breathe on the words and you will begin to connect truth with other truths, which will bring you into greater wisdom and revelation.

## Declarations and Decrees of Truth

I decree and declare that God has given his angels charge over me to protect me from harm.
I decree and declare that I find joy in God's presence—basking in His love and returning my love to Him.
I decree and declare that my life is rich with godly wisdom because I love it and search for it with all my heart.

# Day 31: Love Me by Following Me in Obedience

"Loving me empowers you to obey my commands."
John 14:15 TPT

**1 John 5:1, Hebrews 11:7, 2 John 1:6, Isaiah 50:4,**
**1 John 2:3-6, 1 Peter 4:8, Matthew 5:43-48**

Beloved child, I have been looking forward to this season with you. I see the obedience you have walked out so far. Continue in this pathway of obedience. Increase our daily communion together and do not let sleepiness rule. When I awaken you, consider it an invitation from the Maker of heaven to mentor you, one on one. What value is this to you? Consider how I can shift your heart and mind with My love and My revelation. Time is precious, and you must make good decisions on how you use your time. Begin to think about structuring your week and make goals to accomplish. Be disciplined to say NO the things that seem good, but aren't my best for you. The enemy wants to cleverly steal your time with distractions. The more consistently you lay your day before Me every morning, the more I will show you. The "more" in My kingdom follows after footsteps of obedience. My love carries your heart so that insults don't offend you. Let my mercy overflow from your heart until it overwhelms those who may not deserve it, according to the standards of the world. This gets people's attention. Do not stop loving people everywhere you go.

### Declarations and Decrees of Truth

I decree and declare that God's love is over me like a banner that gives me covering and victory, leading me in the way I should go.
I decree and declare that as God pours his unfailing love upon me every day, I am able to love others freely.
I decree and declare that I am full of hope when I think of my glorious future in Christ.
I decree and declare that I choose Joy. My JOY comes from the Lord.

# DAY 32: I HAVE CHOSEN THIS GENERATION

"Go therefore and make disciples of all nations, baptizing them in the name of the Father and of the Son and of the Holy Spirit, teaching them to observe all that I have commanded you. And behold, I am with you always, to the end of the age." Matthew 28:19-20 ESV

**Ephesians 1:7-10, Isaiah 43:18-19, Jeremiah 31:3**

Beloved child, a great shift is coming to my church. I pre-ordained the shift before the foundation of the world. I have chosen this generation to usher in the greatest harvest of souls anyone has ever imagined. The other revivals through the last few hundreds of years were only a warm-up. This is the generation that will change the world on a large scale—by fulfilling My original commission: to "go and make disciples of nations, baptizing them in My name and teaching them all I have commanded you." There are many of My sons and daughters who I am raising up in this hour. Many who are obscure will be ushered into the light, not by men, but by Me. I know who I have chosen… those with humble hearts and who've set their hearts on intimacy with Me are those I will raise up. These are the ones who walk in My shadow and will go where I go. This last harvest of souls will look nothing like previous revivals. See, I am doing a new thing. Those who tap into My spirit will be aligned with My heart in these last days. Those with their own agendas and plans will be left behind. So, stay close to My presence, child. Follow Me down the road of obedience. I love you with an everlasting love. You are My beloved and I am yours.

## Declarations and Decrees of Truth

I decree and declare that I reflect Jesus Christ, who is the brightness of the glory of God.

I decree and declare that my head has been lifted high above my enemies, and my feet are set up on the solid rock.

I decree and declare that my ears are in tune with what the Lord is saying, in Jesus' name.

# Day 33: My Love is Steadfast

"The steadfast love of the Lord never ceases; his mercies never come to an end; they are new every morning; great is your faithfulness." Lamentations 3:22-23 ESV

**Psalm 24, Song of Songs 2:10-14 TPT, Psalm 42:7-8, 2 Peter 1:2-4, Luke 10:19, Isaiah 42:6-7, Song of Songs 7:9, 8:6**

Beloved, my bride. Open the doors! Fling open the gates, for the Lord goes before you into new places. Trust Me, for My steadfast love surrounds you. New wisdom and knowledge await My faithful ones who are obedient to My commands. Blessing and rewards come in the form of deeper revelation of Me and My love… higher realms in My kingdom… and promotion. Walk with Me to the mountaintop, where we can gaze into the future of My love for My bride. My plans for you are higher than you have understood. The way forward is easy when you are in full communion with Me. Let's practice this today. I have so much to tell you… secrets. A kiss. A kiss of My love. Come away with Me, My darling. All My love is yours. Come bask in My waterfalls… there, you will go deeper with Me — where deep calls out to deep, from My heart to yours. You to Me are like a rose in bloom that I love to pick and show off to everyone around. Your humility is a beautiful piece of the masterpiece I am painting within you.

I am creating in your heart a flame of fire. As My Spirit begins to breathe into your life, this flame will increase and spread to many, until I have an army of burning ones — burning with the glory of the Lord. You are a partaker of My divine nature and I have given you My authority to walk over serpents and scorpions. Look at Me, dear one. Continue to look at Me. Don't look at others. Only Me. I am jealous for you. I want your total devotion. You are My beloved — My sweetest garden, My divine bride and companion. Flow with Me in the spirit. Turn your delightful affection toward Me constantly. Bring your thoughts back to Me — the lover of your soul, your Savior, your Bridegroom. After every conversation, come back to Me. I gaze at you, and those truly faithful to this covenant love… to see if you will meet My eyes again.

## Declarations and Decrees of Truth

I decree and declare that new ideas, inventions, and cures to diseases will come forth in Jesus' name.

I decree and declare that I am a lover of God and nothing can separate me from His love.

# Day 34: Stay in Sync with My Heart

"Here's the one thing I crave from God, the one thing I seek above all else: I want the privilege of living with him every moment in his house, finding the sweet loveliness of his face, filled with awe, delighting in his glory and grace. I want to live my life so close to him that he takes pleasure in my every prayer." Psalm 27:4 TPT

**Psalm 32:7, Isaiah 55:11, Ephesians 5:30-32, Luke 5:33-39, Matthew 5:11-12, James 4:10, 2 Corinthians 10:5, 1 Peter 2:9, Deuteronomy 29:29, 2 Corinthians 3:17-18, Romans 12:1-2**

Today I am holding you in my arms. I surround you with songs of victory, even during the trials you have walked through. I was with you, giving you help to stand on My promises. My promises never fail. Let me carry you across the threshold of the next season because, as my bride, I love you. I am introducing you to new wine and a new wineskin. Expandability and flexibility to My plans and ideas will be key. Wisdom and strategy will come as you focus on My voice and listen. You are my laid-down lover and I see your surrender. Do not harbor offense toward others—but forgive them. Take captive negative thoughts and put them before Me. They will bow and flee.

Communion with us is key to increased intimacy, direction, and blueprints for the next season. Stay pure and bring everything that ushers in guilt to your heart straight to Me in repentance. Our divine love connection must stay flowing. I love you and gaze back at you with unadulterated focus and desire. You are Mine forever. As you sit with Me, I will reveal secrets. Remember, who I call, I equip and transform. Nothing will be impossible for My sons and daughters. In this season, many will experience the reality of who I am. You are a part of a special generation: *The Called Ones*. They have burning hearts, who understand who they are in Christ. This special remnant is called by me to set in motion this great harvest. The key to their motion is intimacy. Staying in sync with My heart, My plans, and My Spirit will be paramount. This move will not come about with man's carefully devised plans. My flames of fire will have wisdom and revelation, straight from the mouth of the Lord. Abide in Me and lean on Me. I need full dependency, which is connected with true humility. Humility is not weakness. It's going low to serve in strength.

## Declarations and Decrees of Truth

I decree and declare that I have the mind of Christ because Christ is in me.

I decree and declare that I have communion and with God through the Holy Spirit.

_____

_____

_____

_____

_____

_____

_____

_____

_____

_____

_____

_____

_____

_____

_____

_____

# Day 35: I Rejoice over You

*"The Lord your God in your midst, the Mighty One, will save; He will rejoice over you with gladness, He will quiet you with His love, He will rejoice over you with singing."*
Zephaniah 3:17 NKJV

**Ephesians 1:3-14, Luke 22:39-46, John 7:38-39, John 15:5, 2 Timothy 2:19, Philippians 2:6-11, 1 John 2:6, John 14:12**

Oh, how I rejoiced the day you were born! Finally, a generation I foreknew before the foundation of the world is coming forth to manifest the Kingdom of God on earth and demonstrate My gospel and power. My Son, eternally God, humbly became a man to live as we originally intended mankind to live… in perfect holiness and in full communion with Me all the time. Jesus showed you perfect love as He laid down His life and all submission to Me so you all could live with us forever. It was a rescue mission. In the garden, the night before His death, I strengthened Him to fulfill His mission and His calling. His eyes were on Me, the Father of all. In the same way, I wish to fill and strengthen all who come to Me in intimate fellowship, who seek to do My will and not their own. This last generation will be different from all the ones who've come before. You are My beloved sons and daughters who believe Me and will demonstrate this gospel with my love. Cling to My beloved Son as He is your vine and life source and will cause you to bear much fruit.

## Declarations and Decrees of Truth

I decree and declare that I have the authority to work miracles in the name of JESUS, as I follow Him in faith and obedience to the Holy Spirit.
I decree and declare that the Lord is everything I need, and He dwells inside of me.
I decree and declare that I believe in Jesus and will do the same works He did and even greater works, as I surrender to the Father's will. (John 14:12)

# Day 36: Fully Surrender to Me

"Seek the Kingdom of God above all else, and live righteously, and he will give you everything you need."
Matthew 6:33 NLT

**Song of Songs 6:2-3, Psalm 16:11, John 17:3 TPT, Matthew 5:8, Hebrews 12:1-2, James 1:19-25, 2 Corinthians 5:21, Genesis 1:27-28, 1 Corinthians 3:16, 1 Corinthians 12, Galatians 5:22**

Beloved, My heart's desire is you. To walk with you among the lilies. You are beginning to realize the level of relationship I desire. I want your whole heart. Fullness of joy awaits those who press in and push past distractions and flashy things the devil plants to detour your heart. Those who come closer and listen step by step will have more and more revelation of who I AM. They will experientially know Me. Those with a pure heart and clean hands will set their eyes on Me and see Me. So throw off every sin that easily entangles and walk with Me, hand in hand. Sin is a choice, it is not inevitable. Full surrender is surely the way to crush this roadblock in your life. Sin is a roadblock to fruitfulness. The enemy would like My people to stay captive to habitual sins, but if you seek first My kingdom and My righteousness, you can make new habits! Habits that drive you closer to Me and further from sin. Move with Me, one step at a time, in forward motion: eyes on Me and ears listening... doing my Word. This is the pathway to a life of victory.

This purity that has been imputed to you, My child, looks beautiful on you. Because Jesus gave everything for you to be made righteous and holy, you can come close to me. You have not only been renewed – but restored to my original intent... made in My image, created for full communion with Me. My sons and daughters were designed to rule and reign with Me on earth. I am limitless and I live within you. This provides full access to the gifts of the Spirit and the fruits of the Spirit. Gifts are given, but fruit is developed. It is a process to see the fruit of the Spirit grow. It is not grown through striving, but through surrender.

## Declarations and Decrees of Truth

I decree and declare that I will fix my eyes on Jesus and throw the lies I hear from the enemy to the foot of the cross.
I decree and declare that I will respond to confrontation with love and mercy.

_____

_____

_____

_____

_____

_____

_____

_____

_____

_____

_____

_____

_____

_____

_____

_____

# Day 37: I Am a Way Maker

"Forget the former things; do not dwell on the past. See, I am doing a new thing! Now it springs up; do you not perceive it? *I am making a way* in the wilderness and streams in the wasteland." Isaiah 43:18-19 NIV

**Matthew 19:26, Psalm 18:16-28, Psalm 147:11, Matthew 11:28, Psalm 24:10 NLT, Isaiah 6:3, Psalm 139:11-12, Psalm 46:10**

Beloved, there is no situation I can't change. The enemy presents you with hopelessness, but I make a way where there is no way. This is why you must keep your eyes on Me. When you look around at the sin and darkness — doubt festers. I hold your heart. I know you feel as though you're being pulled in different directions and about to fall, but don't fear. I see where you stand. Your obedience to Me is a delight, and I am a rewarder of those who diligently seek Me. Your faithfulness is a virtue I treasure. I have set your feet upon a rock: the rock of your salvation. You have a firm foundation, so no matter how your feelings soar out of control, you're not out of control… I am with you and I am the God of miracles. Do not believe what you see and feel, because sometimes feelings can throw you off track. Dive into My Word and abide in Me and My truth. Believe Me over your situation and speak My plans into existence. This is faith. My love reaches well beyond the shroud of darkness. Even the darkness is light to Me. Lay down these burdens you carry and give them to Me. I am the God of armies of angels. Prayer is KEY. Partner with me and agree with ME. Do not forsake speaking truth and freedom over My people. Doing nothing is to align with defeat. Be still and remember who I AM.

## Declarations and Decrees of Truth

I decree and declare that my God will make a way even though the natural situations that look impossible because I put my trust in Him.
I decree and declare that I am aligning with the truth of the Word concerning my identity in Christ.

# DAY 38: COME AWAY WITH ME

"Pay attention and come closer to me, and hear, that
your total being may flourish. I will enter into an
everlasting covenant with you, and I will show
you the same faithful love that I showed David."
Isaiah 55:3 TPT

**Luke 21:28, 1 Corinthians 13:8, John 10, 1 Peter 5:5-7,
2 Corinthians 5:17-20, Matthew 18:18, Song of Solomon 8:14**

Dear child, look up for your redemption draws nigh. My love is never-ending, never-failing, and strong enough to overcome all evil and win back any lost heart. Hear Me, My precious one, hold tight to My voice. Hold tight to My Word. Hold tight to My Spirit. Trust Me. My hand is upon you. My Spirit wind is about to blow. Whom I call I equip. Turn to Me in every available moment and in humility, remain in My love with teachability. Be willing to go low.… like I did. Leaders are servants. Leaders boost others up to see who they are and to see from the mountaintops. They also walk in the valley a lot with those who are captive, until they are freed by the power of My name. You are my ambassador—one who believes Me for heavenly realities to be implemented and utilized on earth. Whatever you loose on earth will be loosed in heaven. Those who know My heart can effectively communicate it and demonstrate My love. Come away with Me daily and I will continue to reveal Myself to you. This is intimacy: A love so deep it is experienced, not just spoken of. I love you, beloved child.

## Declarations and Decrees of Truth

I decree and declare that I am an ambassador of the gospel, and I am created to demonstrate His love to the world.
I decree and declare that I am a man/woman of humility and will go low to serve someone today.
I decree and declare that nothing will hinder my praise and worship before God.

# Day 39: Trust Me as Little Children

"Jesus called a little one to his side and said to them, "Learn this well: Unless you dramatically change your way of thinking and become teachable, and learn about heaven's kingdom realm with the wide-eyed wonder of a child, you will never be able to enter in. Whoever continually humbles himself to become like this gentle child is the greatest one in heaven's kingdom realm." Matthew 18:2-4

**Isaiah 55:8-9, Matthew 9:13, Matthew 25:34-36, Luke 14:13-14, John 15:1-17 TPT, John 14:6, Philippians 4:19, Ephesians 3:20**

This generation is on my heart. I am opening eyes to see who I am, beloved. My ways are not your ways, but My heart still delights in spending time with you to reveal Myself to you. I desire mercy, not sacrifice. Compassion for the hurting, not legalism. Open your eyes to the unseen people around you. Those who are disregarded, that many look past, are valuable to me. And the children…bring the little ones to me. They are precious in My sight. Many see them as a burden (even in my church). Some consider the children's ministry to be *babysitting*. But I tell you, unless adults learn how to become like one of these little precious ones, you won't be able to understand My ways or My kingdom. Just as I was fully dependent on My Father in all I said and did through full communion with Him, so should you be fully dependent on Me. I am your source of life, strength, power, and love. I gave you My righteousness. You cannot live this life for Me on your own strength. Let go of independence. Depend on Me and abide. As a tiny child depends on his mom for everything, so likewise do with Me. I am the Way, the Truth, and the Life. Cling to Me like a branch clings to a vine for sustenance. Without Me, you can do nothing. Let Me empower you with supernatural grace to walk on water with Me in this season. Hold My hand, beloved, and trust Me.

## Declarations and Decrees of Truth

I decree and declare that I will experience joy in the Lord because I trust in Him.

I decree and declare that I will only speak life over myself and others because my words have power.

_____

_____

_____

_____

_____

_____

_____

_____

_____

_____

_____

_____

_____

_____

_____

_____

# Day 40: I Am Your Strong Support

"Do not fear, for I am with you, do not be afraid, for I
am your God; I will strengthen you, I will help you,
I will uphold you with my victorious right hand."
Isaiah 41:10 NSRV

**Luke 6:35-36, Luke 22:41-44, Ephesians 6:13-14, 2 Corinthians 10:5,
Hebrews 12:2, 2 Chronicles 16:9, Romans 12:2, 1 Peter 2:24,
Matthew 11:28, Psalm 78:35, Psalm 61:2**

Look at Me beloved... you are beautiful to Me. Give yourself
to love, even when it is a sacrifice. This is what My Son did. Jesus
loved all, despite how they treated Him. He was so confident
in Me and My love for Him that I was all He needed. The Spirit
spoke and strengthened Him during extremely difficult times.
STAND. Stand on My promises to you. Bask in My love. My love
is a waterfall pouring over your life. I see every difficulty. Each
time, I lean forward to see if you turn your thoughts toward Me
so I can strengthen you with the truth, dismantling the lies the
enemy is trying to form in your mind. You must look at Me. My
eyes run to and fro, over all the earth, toward all my sons and
daughters to strengthen those who are fully surrendered, laid-
down lovers, making their lives to be living sacrifices. I have My
eyes on you, beloved one. Lean back into My embrace.

You are not alone, because My Spirit goes with you wherever you go. In this season, it is imperative you walk very close
to Me. Just be still with Me as you drive in the car. Use the time
on your drive to worship and listen to my logos and rhema
word. You are so precious to Me. No word I have spoken to
you have I changed my mind about, pertaining to your future.
You are chosen. The enemy desperately wants you to bleed
emotionally, but I am a father of restoration. Let me heal your
wounds. I am your healer. Spend MORE time listening to Me.
Bring to Me every burden and allow Me to give you peace
and rest in exchange. I am your Father, your best friend, your
Comforter. Bring everything before Me. Hurt that is bottled
up will fester. Let Me pour My healing water and oil over this
wound in your heart. You are My child, part of My bride, and
My friend. I am your strong support. Lean on Me when you're
not strong and I'll be the rock you need to stand on. And when

the lies and darts come… you can stand. Stand on My truth because My love is strong for you.

## Declarations and Decrees of Truth

I decree and declare that my health is being restored to me and I receive healing for the wounds in my heart.

_____

_____

_____

_____

_____

_____

_____

_____

_____

_____

_____

_____

_____

_____

_____

_____

# DAY 41: I AM YOUR ANCHOR

"So it is impossible for God to lie for we know that his promise and his vow will never change! And now we have run into his heart to hide ourselves in his faithfulness. This is where we find his strength and comfort, for he empowers us to seize what has already been established ahead of time—an unshakeable hope! We have this certain hope like a strong, *unbreakable anchor* holding our souls to God himself. Our anchor of hope is fastened to the mercy seat which sits in the heavenly realm beyond the sacred threshold, and where Jesus, our forerunner, has gone in before us." Hebrews 6:18-20 TPT

**Psalm 23, Jeremiah 29:13, Deuteronomy 30:19-20, John 10:27, Romans 8:1, 1 John 1:9, Ephesians 5:25-26, 2 Corinthians 2:14, Isaiah 11:2**

Beloved sons and daughters, hold fast to My love. My love is an anchor that holds tightly to those who believe. Trust in Me to speak and to lead you in paths of righteousness for My name's sake. I have so much to tell you. Draw close to Me and you will begin to hear the love I am speaking over you. The more you listen, the more you will hear and recognize the voice of your Father, who loves you. I want to pour My love over you every day like a waterfall. When you seek Me, you will find Me. I delight in your affection. My eyes range to and fro across the earth, looking for those whose hearts are loyal to Me. I will strengthen you and breathe life into you. I am the voice of truth pouring over you like rivers of living water. When the enemy of your soul comes toward you with thoughts of condemnation, shame, and regret, take your thoughts captive and make them obedient to Jesus. Do not come into agreement with the lies he brings. Believe Me, your Abba father, that you are loved, forgiven, empowered by My Holy Spirit, and victorious over the enemy, because you belong to Me. Jesus has paid it all for you. His life was laid down so that you could live with Me forever, as sons and daughters.

## Declarations and Decrees of Truth

I decree and declare that today I will take every thought captive that does not align with truth about my identity in Christ and cast the lies down, in Jesus' name.

I decree and declare that I am filled and empowered by the Spirit of wisdom and understanding, the Spirit of counsel and might, and the Spirit of knowledge and the fear of the Lord. (Isaiah 11:2)

_____

_____

_____

_____

_____

_____

_____

_____

_____

_____

_____

_____

_____

_____

# Day 42: I AM the God of the Breakthrough!

David asked God, "Should I attack the Philistines? Will you help me win?" The Lord told David, "Yes, attack them! I will give you victory." David and his army marched to Baal-Perazim, where they attacked and defeated the Philistines. He said, "I defeated my enemies because God broke through them like a mighty flood." So he named the place "The Lord Broke Through."
1 Chronicles 14:10-11 CEV

**Psalm 42:7-11, Isaiah 52:7, James 4:8, Matthew 11:28, James 1:21-25, Ephesians 5:1, Proverbs 3:5-6, Matthew 19:26, Exodus 3:13-15, Romans 4:17, Ephesians 6:11-13**

Beloved one of My heart, how beautiful are your feet on the mountain... bringing my good news. Your desire to live for Me and please Me is noticed by Me, My child. I'm so near to you. I want to restore your heart's wounds. Come to Me. Look completely into My eyes and I will give you rest. Herein lies the peace you seek — even as the situations around you are in turmoil. Let your eyes meet My steady gaze. I heard your cries and I am your defender. I am moving mountains looming before you, because I am the Prince of Peace and the King of your heart.

Beloved, become My Word. Live in love. My love will manifest through you, within your sacrifice of self. Although you cannot see or imagine how things around you will work out, trust these situations to Me. Commit them to Me and lay them down. In your surrender and yielding, they become Mine to breathe My supernatural love upon and freedom into. Remember, raising the dead to life is impossible with man, but it's My specialty. Show Me your trust. Lay your burdens down. Let go of fear, dread, and worry, because those are the enemy's tactics. Don't fall into his traps. Fully align yourself with My ability to break the bonds of wickedness. I said to Moses, "I AM WHO I AM." I am still *I AM* today and for all times. Declare love and forgiveness to reign in all of the hearts in the difficult situations of your life. I am reuniting people and healing disunity in this hour. Call it into being, beloved. Stand. Believe Me, not the natural problems you are facing. I am the God of the breakthrough.

## Declarations and Decrees of Truth

I decree and declare that I am triumphant over my obstacles because God gives me the victory.

I decree and declare that turmoil in my life will become overwhelmed by the peace of God.

_____

_____

_____

_____

_____

_____

_____

_____

_____

_____

_____

_____

_____

_____

# DAY 43: MY LOVE IS OUTRAGEOUS

"Come to me with your ears wide open. Listen, and you will find life. I will make an everlasting covenant with you. I will give you all the unfailing love I promised to David". Isaiah 55:3 NLT

**John 17:3, 20-26, Hebrews 11:6, 2 Corinthians 3:18, 1 Corinthians 12:7-11, Philippians 3:12, Proverbs 2:6, Romans 10:17, 1 John 3:8, 1 John 3:1, Isaiah 55, John 15:13**

Dear one, I see your desire to know Me more deeply, and you will have what you ask. Blessed is he or she who seeks to know me with all their heart. As My obedient child, in this next season, you will see astounding miracles begin to manifest all around you. The key is intimacy with Me through My Spirit… just as My Son had as He walked in love on earth. Demonstrate my goodness on a new level—a level that no eye has seen, or ear has heard. This will be different than past generations because of the technology available. The news of My goodness and mercy will be widely seen.

You must stay close to Me, beloved. If you desire your life to be different from the way it is now, you must change some things you're doing. How can you successfully silence distractions and look to Me all through your day? Stay in conversation with Me through the eyes and ears of your heart. Connect your heart to Mine consciously. Bring your affection to Me in one thought. Believe what I say, instead of what you see with your eyes. I am looking for courageous ambassadors who will step into faith (and risk), performing my rhema word as I speak to them. Press in for more and more words of knowledge from me. Ask me. You will be amazed at the flowing river of knowledge about everyone you encounter, just waiting to be tapped into. My love for every person is outrageous. I am pursuing hearts as we speak. Come with Me, and when you "feel" that you're not feeling it—press in, because the enemy is a manipulator of feelings. Ask Me, listen, and together we will destroy the works of the devil. Speak when I tell you to speak. Love well. Loving in the face of persecution or opposition unravels the enemy's schemes. I will give you strength in those moments... when love is a sacrifice. Nothing is unseen by Me. I see that you're becoming more and more like Jesus. Come close to me and rest in my peace. I am holding on to every detail of your life. Abide, My child.

## Declarations and Decrees of Truth

I decree and declare that God's presence fills me up to overflow as I go through my day, loving people with His love.

_____

_____

_____

_____

_____

_____

_____

_____

_____

_____

_____

_____

_____

_____

_____

# Day 44: I AM Your Bridegroom

"In the same way the church is devoted to Christ, let the wives be devoted to their husbands in everything. And to the husbands, you are to demonstrate love for your wives with the same tender devotion that Christ demonstrated to us, his bride. For he died for us, sacrificing himself to make us holy and pure, cleansing us through the showering of the pure water of the Word of God. *All that he does in us is designed* to make us a mature church for his pleasure, until we become a source of praise to him—glorious and radiant, beautiful and holy, without fault or flaw... For this reason, a man is to leave his father and his mother and lovingly hold to his wife, since the two have become joined as one flesh. Marriage is the beautiful design of the Almighty, a great and sacred mystery—*meant to be a vivid example* of Christ and his church."
Ephesians 5:25-27, 31-32 TPT

**Song of Songs 7:1-9 TPT, Isaiah 62:5TPT, Matthew 10:27, John 3:28-29, Luke 9:2, Acts 9:26-28, John 15:4 TPT, Proverbs 16:3, Luke 22:42, Jeremiah 18:3-4, Luke 5:33-39, Isaiah 54:5, Isaiah 61:1-3, Acts 7:55-56**

You are my bride, a special part of the bride of Christ. Your life stands tall and shines bright. When you open your mouth in conversations to others, tell them of our love. Tell them of My love and My sacrifice for them. Beloved, such a great season is coming. The way you prepare is to come close to Me in intimate communion. I will tell you many secrets. In a healthy marriage, husbands and wives keep nothing back from each other. And the more time you make for each other, the more you can share and know even the deepest secrets of each other's hearts. So it will be between Me and My bride. Talk to Me about everything. I wish to lead you in my divine ways. It's part of full surrender to bring all your decisions to Me. Commit your way to Me and I will give you the desires of your heart. I laid My own will aside to do My Father's will. Are you willing to do this also?

Without friction and pressing, a lump of clay would never be made into a masterpiece vase displaying the beauty that it was created to display. I've been making new wine, beloved. The crushing and pressing were allowed in the pursuit of growing you into My magnum opus. No suffering or trial is ever in vain. I turn all the ashes into beauty. You are so beautiful to Me. My love for you vanquishes all your enemies. Do not doubt My power to exonerate those close to you who are bound. Keep your eyes fixed on Me. If you hold My hand and walk beside Me, you'll never go the wrong direction. Put all your trust in Me. I love you.

## Declarations and Decrees of Truth

I decree and declare that I will walk in full communion with my Bridegroom, Jesus.

_____

_____

_____

_____

_____

_____

_____

_____

_____

_____

_____

_____

_____

# Day 45: I AM your Beloved Creator

"You formed my innermost being, shaping my delicate inside and my intricate outside, and wove them all together in my mother's womb. You saw who you created me to be before I became me! Before I'd ever seen the light of day, the number of days you planned for me were already recorded in your book. Every single moment you are thinking of me! How precious and wonderful to consider that you cherish me constantly in your every thought! O God, your desires toward me are more than the grains of sand on every shore!" Psalm 139:13, 16-18 TPT

**Ephesians 3:18-19, Ecclesiastes 11:5, Isaiah 40:28, Isaiah 51:7,12, Galatians 1:10, Deuteronomy 31:6, Proverbs 3:5-6, Jeremiah 33:3, Isaiah 40:28-31**

Beloved one of My heart, your children are so very precious to Me. They were Mine before they were yours—as you were Mine before you were your parents'. My love stretches far beyond your understanding. I go with each child today and I never leave them alone. Teach them that they should never base their worth on what their friends say or think about them. If you live by the praises of people, you'll die by their criticism. Understand the truth: you have been created intricately by Me, the CREATOR. I hung every star in the universe and knit you perfectly together in your mother's womb. You are so valuable to Me. I have dreamed a destiny for your life that matches perfectly how I created you. Trust in Me; My plans for you are great and My thoughts for you outnumber the grains of sand on the seashore. You are My beloved child. Turn your ear to Me and I will tell you of My love.

## Declarations and Decrees of Truth

I decree and declare that God's promises for me and my family are YES and AMEN.

I decree and declare that my character will align with the Word of God.

I decree and declare that my destiny is extremely important to my Father in Heaven and He will see it through to completion.

# Day 46: My Love Defends You

"So I kneel humbly in awe before the Father of our Lord Jesus, the Messiah, the perfect Father of every father and child in heaven and on the earth. And I pray that he would unveil within you the unlimited riches of his glory and favor until supernatural strength floods your innermost being with his divine might and explosive power. Then, by constantly using your faith, the life of Christ will be released deep inside you, and the resting place of his love will become the very source and root of your life." Ephesians 3:14-17 TPT

**Ephesians 1:14 TPT, Psalm 18, Ephesians 6:10-13, Romans 4:13-21, John 15:7-9, 2 Chronicles 20:1-30, Isaiah 41:10**

My devoted one, stand on my hope-promise. I am standing beside you and nothing catches Me off guard. I am your defender. But sometimes I teach you how to fight in the battle through prayer. Declare and decree your faith is in My power. My power has put every enemy under your feet in victory. As you commune with Me: THE LIVING GOD, you will walk with Me and see this reality enforced when you see a breakthrough in the natural. With a surrendered communing heart, your destiny is secure. Believe in Me, not your circumstances. My ways are higher, and I can see past the fog you are currently standing in. Fix your eyes on Me because I know the way. Grab My hand, dear one, My love washes you and makes you whole. I am moving behind the scenes for you, and I'm strengthening you with peace and My glorious presence. Sing praises for My provision and deliverance even before you witness the manifestation. That's faith.

### Declarations and Decrees of Truth

I decree and declare that God's power flows through me like rivers of living water.
I decree and declare that any fear of the supernatural is broken right now in my life.
I decree and declare that I will NOT FEAR, for my strong and mighty God defends me.

# Day 47: Let the Living Hope Shine through You

"Blessed be the God and Father of our Lord Jesus Christ!
According to his great mercy, he has caused us to be born
again to a living hope through the resurrection of Jesus
Christ from the dead, to an inheritance that is imperishable,
undefiled, and unfading, kept in heaven for you, who by
God's power are being guarded through faith for a salvation
ready to be revealed in the last time." 1 Peter 1:3-5 ESV

**Isaiah 41:13, John 3:34, Romans 4:17, Zephaniah 3:17, Hebrews 13:8,
Romans 15:13, Hebrews 10:23, Romans 5:5, Colossians 1:27**

My beloved, I hold your hand. I am so proud of you for
believing Me over your circumstances... for calling those things
that *are not* as though they are. Faith. I am building inside you
an indispensable faith for what I say, regardless of what is happening in the natural. You must get accustomed to this principle. Try to step out into risk, to what I say... then you will see
it manifest in the natural. This is called trusting your Daddy.
I've been singing over you this morning that Jesus is your
Living Hope. He is your hope yesterday, today, and tomorrow.

Stand up for Me this weekend. Your light shines brightly
in the darkness—don't hide your light. Shine and bring joy
to every circumstance that comes forth from your hope-filled
heart. My promises are true, beloved. You are about to see My
promises manifest. This is an open-door season. Just look at
Me and commune with Me—you're living hope. I will infuse
you with My love, joy, and peace—all of these will overflow
onto those surrounding you. And if you become depleted or
robbed, come get more. The rivers of My presence are yours for
the taking. I give to you without limits. Just come back to Me. I
am jealous for you. My love for you was poured out like wine
and I laid My life down for our full communion today. Heaven
starts now. Give Me your attentive affection and watch what
happens. Ours is a beautiful love story without end.

## Declarations and Decrees of Truth

I decree and declare that the favor of God is undeniable in my life and my family's lives.

I decree and declare that the light of Jesus shines through me everywhere I go.

I decree and declare I rest in the truth that God's protection will keep me from harm.

_____

_____

_____

_____

_____

_____

_____

_____

_____

_____

_____

_____

_____

_____

_____

_____

# Day 48: Great is My Faithfulness

"The steadfast love of the Lord never ceases; his mercies never come to an end; they are new every morning; great is your faithfulness. "The Lord is my portion," says my soul, "therefore I will hope in him." The Lord is good to those who wait for him, to the soul who seeks him. It is good that one should wait quietly for the salvation of the Lord." Lamentations 3:22-26 ESV

**Psalm 37:3, 2 Peter 1:3-4, Psalm 62:7, Isaiah 22:22, Isaiah 43:18-19, Isaiah 55:11, Psalm 139:9 TPT, Psalm 16:8, Psalm 46:1, 2 Corinthians 6:2, Isaiah 60:1-2, Psalm 119:133, Isaiah 30:21**

My beloved child, great is My faithfulness unto you. You are so precious to Me and I am your defender. Part of being your defender is to teach you how to stand and wait, and when to take hold of My promises, with My power. You've been in a time of waiting, but I'm opening new doors in this season. Move in sync with Me. This requires constant communion between us. Listening and obedience will be important. This is a new season, unlike all others you've ever known. Expect new things. Your life won't look like past seasons. There is an increase when you step into faith (and risk) for Me. My Spirit will surround you, strengthen you, and equip you to passionately enforce My Word. My Word does not return void. Declare and decree freedom every day. Come ride on the wings of the dawn with Me and I will show you your firm promises fulfilled. Rejoice in Me, your Father, for you are greatly loved by Me and I hold your future in My hands. Walk with Me, step-by-step, in sync… speak when I tell you to speak and do what I tell you to do and go where I tell you to go. You will see miracles manifest. Your family will be free. Trust in Me, your very-present help in times of trouble. I am your Rock, your Source, the great I AM. And you dear one — are Mine. Continue to proclaim My faithfulness with thanksgiving. This ushers in my presence and glory.

## Declarations and Decrees of Truth

I decree and declare that my decisions will be led by the Holy Spirit; He will direct my steps.

I decree and declare that I will not be shaken by the words of the enemy.

I decree and declare that I will see miracles manifest around me as I step out and pray for people in my path.

_____

_____

_____

_____

_____

_____

_____

_____

_____

_____

_____

_____

_____

_____

_____

_____

# DAY 49: I AM THE ONE WHO HEALS YOUR HEART

"But you are God's chosen treasure—priests who are kings, a spiritual "nation" set apart as God's devoted ones. He called you out of darkness to experience his marvelous light, and now he claims you as his very own. He did this so that you would broadcast his glorious wonders *throughout the world*."
1 Peter 2:9 TPT

**Ephesians 6:11-13, John 8:44, Luke 8:17, 1 John 1:5-7, 1 Peter 1:14-16, Ephesians 5:11, Revelation 2:20-21, Psalm 89:34, Psalm 103:20, Romans 8:26-27, 1 Corinthians 14:14-15, 1 Corinthians 4:5, Jude 1:20-21, Psalm 91:1**

Beloved one, My hand is upon your life. Rest in trust—that I will deliver you from the schemes of the enemy. He has targeted you because of our intimacy. So, press in. I want to give you greater revelation. Speak against the lie that says I've pulled the rug out from under you and left you stranded and alone. Those are lies. I'm simply shining My light on the broken places of my children's lives—so healing can and will take place. Without light, sin stays in the dark and festers. This is the season of exposure. First for my people, then the world. Justice will prevail. Be holy as I am holy. I am stepping on the scene with My Spirit of Truth. I would not expose the truth without a chance to repent. Even Jezebel had that chance.

Claim My promises over the lives of the people you're praying for that need salvation. Jeremiah 24:7 says," I will give him a heart to know me: that I am the Lord. He will be mine and I will be his God, for he will return to me with all of his heart." Until this comes to fruition, continue to fix your eyes on Me in the unseen. I AM truth. My hand is heavy upon you, My child. My angels surround you… obeying the voice of My word. Speak life and speak love. Stand your ground and put on the armor I gave you. Pray in the spirit as much as possible. My Spirit knows what to pray when you have no words. Fall into my arms and rest in my shadow. Freedom is coming for My people.

## Declarations and Decrees of Truth

I decree and declare that God takes pleasure in healing my heart, spirit, and body.

I decree and declare that the Spirit of God lives in me and gives me freedom to love extravagantly, with no strings attached.

I decree and declare that I will experience eternal life today as I seek to KNOW God with all my heart in my secret place.

---

---

---

---

---

---

---

---

---

---

---

---

---

---

# Day 50: Trust Me for Deliverance

"You have built a stronghold by the songs of babies. Strength rises up with the chorus of singing children. This kind of praise has the power to shut Satan's mouth. Childlike worship will silence the madness of those who oppose you." Psalm 8:2 TPT

**Psalm 121:1-8, Psalm 61:3, John 10:28-29, Ephesians 4:26-27, Psalm 91:1-4,14, Psalm 103:10-13, Romans 5:8, Matthew 22:37, 2 Corinthians 5:14-16**

Beloved one, hold your hands up to Me. When your hands are up, worshiping and trusting Me, what else are you able to do but fix your eyes on Me and My glory? Am I bigger than the situation you are facing? Can anyone compare to Me? My wisdom, My power, My ability to break strongholds will cause chains to fall off at a word. I AM… and I AM still. You are so precious to Me. You are Mine. As high as the mountaintops reach to the heavens, My love for you is a strong tower — protecting you from the destruction desired by the evil one. But he cannot snatch you out of My hand. Live holy, pure lives and do not live in compromise. Do not let the devil get a foothold in your life. These sayings are truth: love Me with all your heart and I will overshadow you and protect you from disaster. My hand is upon you. Speak life and deliverance over your family, in full trust that it will be done, as you wait on My divine timing.

This is rest: trusting Me so completely that worry and anxiety have no place to land on your heart. Gaze at Me with eyes of trust, knowing that I never fail. Worship Me and thank Me for My promises which will come to pass. Your family is precious to Me. Remember, I do not treat them as their sins deserve, but as a Father who forgives when asked. While you were in sin, Jesus died for you. See them through My eyes of love. Remember the season when I led you out of fear and deception? This is that season for them. I am merciful and My love heals. Look at Me. Let My presence surround you with a renewed perspective and an attitude of gratitude. I love you.

## Declarations and Decrees of Truth

I decree and declare that I will be diligent and unmoved, despite my circumstances, because my trust is in the Lord.
I decree and declare that my God sees me and is working behind the scenes in my favor.

_____

_____

_____

_____

_____

_____

_____

_____

_____

_____

_____

_____

_____

_____

_____

_____

# Day 51: Focus Your Mind and Heart on Me

Jesus told him, "I am the way, the truth, and the life. No one can come to the Father except through me". John 14:6 NKJV

**Ephesians 1:5-7, Psalm 46:10, Song of Songs 7:12, Psalm 139:16, Isaiah 43:2, Psalm 7:17, Psalm 23:5, Isaiah 26:3 NKJV, Luke 10:19, John 7:37, Zephaniah 3:17, 2 Corinthians 3:18**

Child of mine, because you gave your life to me, you are, indeed, accepted through My beloved Son. You don't have to strive to please Me, you already do. You're beautiful to Me. Run with Me to the vineyard of My love where the fruit grows in abundance and you are secure in who I have created you to be. No one can change this. I created you for an incredible purpose. I knew you before you were born. I knew all the things you would walk through, yet not be burned. You are My beloved and I want you to keep your eyes on Me and your focus on your Living Hope. I am strong and mighty to save, crushing your enemies. When your eyes lock on Me in praise and thanksgiving, your enemies can't even come close to knocking you down, even when you're seated at the table with them. Their words cannot penetrate your heart, when your heart is stayed on Me. When you are in full alignment and agreement with the truth, the enemy can have no power over you. He stays under your feet. Any lie that comes, toss it out and laugh with Me. Your enemy is a withering branch because My blood won the victory. It is finished. My gospel stands for all time.

## Declarations and Decrees of Truth

I decree and declare that I can do ALL THINGS through Christ who gives me strength.
I decree and declare that my time will not be wasted.
I decree and declare that salvation is coming to everyone in my house.

# Day 52: Rest in my Presence

"Are you tired? Worn out? Burned out on religion? Come to me. Get away with me and you'll recover your life. I'll show you how to take a real rest. Walk with me and work with me—watch how I do it. Learn the unforced rhythms of grace. I won't lay anything heavy or ill-fitting on you. Keep company with me and you'll learn to live freely and lightly."
Matthew 11:28-30 MSG

**2 Corinthians 3:17, Proverbs 18:21, Matthew 4:19, 1 Peter 5:7, Titus 2:7-8, John 7:37-39, 1 Corinthians 6:19-20, Romans 8:11, Colossians 2:9, Acts 1:8, John 10:10**

Beloved, speak and declare freedom and wholeness and holiness for your hurting friends and family, every day, until you see a shift. Believe Me and My Word over your circumstances. Calmly rest in my presence. Don't take the enemy's invitation to anxiety and becoming flustered. Rest in your Father's love. I AM THE WAY. Follow My lead. Those in your life are watching your walk. Spirits tell you to shrink back in fear, but instead live out loud, in love. With mercy and grace on the tip of your tongue, speak life because it brings life. Ask Me to fill you, to replenish the living water you're freely giving away. You do not go alone because I am with you always. Heighten your awareness of My Spirit in your car and as you go into public places. Be aware that you are a carrier of My glory and presence. I am always waiting for you to turn your affection toward Me. When your thoughts wander, capture them and bring them back to Me. Focus your mind and heart toward the One who longs to cradle you in His arms all throughout your day. My love is strong enough to vanquish every enemy that comes against you. I am standing with you. You are never alone. Lean into Me, beloved and give Me your full trust. I know all things and I know what you need. What the devil has tried to destroy in your life, I am making beautiful.

## Declarations and Decrees of Truth

I decree and declare that this is a time of renewing our strength and soaring in His presence.

I decree and declare that I am a minister of reconciliation to offset injustices and bring healing to people everywhere I go, in Jesus' name.

_____

_____

_____

_____

_____

_____

_____

_____

_____

_____

_____

_____

_____

_____

_____

_____

# Day 53: My Goodness is Yours

"Drink deeply of the pleasures of God. Experience for yourself the joyous mercies he gives to all who turn to hide themselves in him. Worship in awe and wonder, all you who've been made holy! For all who fear him will feast with plenty. Even the strong and the wealthy grow weak and hungry, but those who passionately pursue the Lord will never lack any good thing." Psalm 34:8-10 TPT

**Psalm 31:19, Galatians 5:1, Jeremiah 29:13, Ephesians 5:13-14, Psalm 139:1-24, Psalm 107:10-16 TPT, John 8:32, 1 Peter 2:9**

Beloved one, I have goodness in store for you right around the bend. You'll see it, for My mercy never fails. My heart for you exceeds anything you've seen or measured. I see how you yearn for Me, to know Me. Therefore, I will pick you up and bring you close, closer than you've known before. The things of this world will continue to grow dim, but My love and kingdom will rise stronger and higher in your heart. I will be found by you. In your diligent seeking of me, our intimate connection will grow stronger and you will see My Word performed. My goodness will brighten the darkening culture. It will expose many sins and, when combined with my extreme love, it will bring many to repentance and transformation. Many in the body of Christ don't know intimacy with Me is possible. Many don't feel worthy enough to try to connect with Me because of the lies they believe. I will empower you to speak the TRUTH of My Word and break the yokes and chains. Bondage from lies will be crushed in this season. I am calling My sons and daughters home. I am waiting with open arms to hold them and commune with them. My love reaches into the darkness and brings My lost ones into the light of My love and truth. Follow Me into your future where My light is shining brightly.

## Declarations and Decrees of Truth

I decree and declare that I will grow in intimate fellowship with God.
I decree and declare that the spirit of rejection, loneliness, and abandonment will not grip my heart.

I decree and declare that I am a lover of God and nothing can separate me from His love.

_____

_____

_____

_____

_____

_____

_____

_____

_____

_____

_____

_____

_____

_____

_____

_____

# DAY 54: ARISE

"My beloved spoke and said to me, "*Arise*, my darling, my beautiful one, come with me." Song of Songs 2:10

"*Arise*, shine; For your light has come! And the glory of the Lord is risen upon you. For behold, the darkness shall cover the earth, and deep darkness the people; but the Lord will arise over you, and His glory will be seen upon you." Isaiah 60:1-2 NKJV

**Revelation 19:6-8, Isaiah 54:5,17, Romans 8:14, Acts 4:29-31, Ephesians 1:11-14, Luke 8:16-18**

My bride, it is time for you to ARISE. You have been learning about the foundational key for following Me: intimacy with your Source of life. As you move forward, all uncharted waters will be exciting, but not fearful, when you are led by Me. I will direct your steps. I will speak through you as you yield to My Holy Spirit. Move in sync together with Me—like a hand in a glove. There will be miracles, signs, and wonders in this next season and many people out of church and even in the church will run to Me… to know Me. Many Christians will realize they do not really know Me—they only know ABOUT Me, more like an acquaintance than a friend. Understanding My true gospel and who I am, as well as who they are, will be a paramount priority. My people must see that they are children with a great inheritance.

Let your faithfulness to our communion be head-turning. Come closer to Me, and rest in My shadow. My love is vast, and it vanquishes your enemies. My revelation-light makes everything visible and heals the cracks you didn't even realize you had. My desire is wholeness for My sons and daughters on fire for Me. You were created to burn and catch others on fire as my spirit-wind blows. My life shines through you. Although there will always be opposition to My kingdom on this side of heaven, you can walk on water with Me and learn how to STAND in My authority to pushback this opposition. Identity is an important understanding. Along with intimacy, it's foundational. Arise and shine for Me, everywhere you go!

## Declarations and Decrees of Truth

I decree and declare that the calling on my life will not be compromised, in Jesus' name.

I decree and declare that I will shine the light and love of Jesus everywhere I go.

_____

_____

_____

_____

_____

_____

_____

_____

_____

_____

_____

_____

_____

_____

# Day 55: Deny Yourself and Follow Me

"And calling the crowd to him with his disciples, he said to them, "If anyone would come after me, let him deny himself and take up his cross and follow me."
Mark 8:34 ESV

**Matthew 5:5, Psalm 16:11, Romans 12:1, Galatians 5:16,24, Romans 8:14-17, John 17:3, Song of Songs 8:6-7 TPT, Luke 19:10, Ephesians 1:4, Hebrews 4:15**

Beloved, blessed are the meek for they will inherit the earth. Fullness of joy comes to those who wait upon Me and the inheritance of My promises. The gospel is offensive to many because they are faced with the decision to go the way of the kingdom—which looks like dying to themselves or take their own way—which speaks to their fleshly tendencies. This is why KNOWING ME is the paramount ingredient to the equation. My love, My grace, My kindness, My mercy, and My truth speak to the deepest longings of one's soul... causing them to run into My arms and never want to leave. Over time and in deep relationship, it doesn't even seem like a sacrifice anymore.

I came to seek and save what was lost. I came for you because I love you. Your life was so worth My sacrifice. My sacrifice was a choice I made. Before the foundation of the world, I knew you. I understood in order to rescue My bride, I had to demonstrate My love. I gave all for you. I treasure that time, although it was difficult, because I walked in your shoes. I became one of you. And I went first: I went forth in the power of the Holy Spirit to show you My Father's plan for all of you... to walk with the Father in intimacy, in righteousness, and in power and authority from heaven. This has been bestowed on God's children in order to manifest the kingdom and bring heaven to earth. Step into these as a child of God and as My bride. The Holy Spirit empowers and moves you like a glove fitted on a hand. Then you will be able to do the will of the Father when you surrender to Him fully, as I did. His plans are astoundingly good.

## Declarations and Decrees of Truth

I decree and declare that I count it all joy when I face testing, temptations, and trials because God is making me more like Jesus and will help me overcome.

I decree and declare that I am full of hope as I look forward to the future because God is with me.

_____

_____

_____

_____

_____

_____

_____

_____

_____

_____

_____

_____

_____

_____

_____

# Day 56: You are Partakers of My Divine Nature

"Grace and peace be multiplied to you in the knowledge of God and of Jesus our Lord, as His divine power has given to us all things that pertain to life and godliness, through the knowledge of Him who called us by glory and virtue, by which have been given to us exceedingly great and precious promises, that through these you may be partakers of the divine nature, having escaped the corruption that is in the world through lust." II Peter 1:2-4 NKJV

**Hebrews 4:13, 2 Corinthians 5:21, 2 Corinthians 3:18, Hebrews 11:1,6, Ephesians 6:13, 1 Corinthians 15:58, 1 Corinthians 16:13, Colossians 3:3, Habakkuk 3:3-4 NLT**

My child, I see you. I know your heart and every thought that comes across your mind's canvas. Nothing is hidden from the Creator of all. You have been made fully whole and righteous through the blood of Christ as My child. I am transforming you into the image of My Son, Jesus. I am delighted when I see you take steps to believe Me and My Word over your circumstances in the natural. Faith isn't a concept, it's an *action*. It's fixing your gaze upon Me and saying what I say is truth. Sometimes you must stand. "Standing" can be a lonely place to be, humanly speaking. But you are hidden in Christ with Me, and I am with you. I will be your strength.

The more you decree My truth, the quicker you will see alignments made with heaven on earth. There is power in your words. You are partakers of My divine nature. My power does flow from your hands. When you lay your hands on the sick, envision My power flowing from you into them. Although you may not physically see it, a transfer is occurring. Just believe. You don't need to assess whether you have "faith enough" for a certain need. Ask yourself, "Could my Jesus do this?" After all, We made the stars and told them where to stand. Nothing is impossible with God. Nothing. *All things are possible for he or she who believes.*

## Declarations and Decrees of Truth

I decree and declare that I am the hands and feet of Jesus and I will see miracles as I step out and love people through prayer, in Jesus' name.

I decree and declare that everything is possible for me when I truly believe the power of God flows through my hands as His son or daughter.

I decree and declare that I am a partaker of His divine nature.

_____

_____

_____

_____

_____

_____

_____

_____

_____

_____

_____

_____

_____

_____

# DAY 57: HERE COMES THE HARVEST

Then Jesus explained: "My nourishment comes from doing the will of God, who sent me, and from finishing his work. You know the saying, 'Four months between planting and harvest.' But I say, wake up and look around. The fields are already, ripe for harvest. The harvesters are paid good wages, and the fruit they harvest is people brought to eternal life. What joy awaits both the planter and the harvester alike! You know the saying, 'One plants and another harvests.' And it's true. I sent you to harvest where you didn't plant; others had already done the work, and now you will get to gather the harvest." John 4:35-38 NLT

**Matthew 9:37-38, Galatians 6:9, Psalm 85:12, Mark 4:26-29, Matthew 10:7-8, Matthew 24:14, Isaiah 66:8, Acts 2:17-21, 1 Corinthians 4:20, Luke 10:19, 1 Corinthians 14:1, Proverbs 1:33, Jeremiah 31:3, Proverbs 3:5, Psalm 84:10**

Beloved, My voice in your mind and heart will increase as you focus on Me. Many things will increase in this last season of harvest. The harvest is ripe. And I'm calling My sons and daughters into the harvest field. For everyone who calls on the name of the Lord will be saved. The gospel will be preached through all the world. Nations will be saved in a day. Oh, beloved, great is My love for humanity. I will stretch out My hand and touch many through the army I am building and training. My Spirit is moving, and things will constantly be changing. Set your gaze on Me. I am leading you in many ways… My still, small voice, yes, but also in dreams and visions. My will is moving My sons and daughters into full trust in Me. In complete surrender, they will experience My power flowing through them. You will take authority over sickness and disease, and it will flee in My name. You will speak My words out of your mouth so that My heart is communicated and the person you are speaking to will run to Me and be totally transformed.

Do not fear inadequacy. You are worthy, you are pure, and your value was worth My life's sacrifice. I've heard your cries for more. I always hear the prayers of the righteous and I will answer those prayers. I am the Lord, who guides you on unfamiliar paths and who lights each step you take in obedience. I love you with an everlasting love. I draw My own with loving-kindness. I am the Lord of hosts and My hosts will guard you in all your ways. Be strong and courageous, because I go with you everywhere you go. I am mighty to save. I will not let your foot slip. Better is one day in My courts than a thousand elsewhere.

## Declarations and Decrees of Truth

I decree and declare that I am a harvester, and I will lead many people to Jesus.

_____

_____

_____

_____

_____

_____

_____

_____

_____

_____

_____

_____

_____

# Day 58: Radical Love, Radical Generosity, Radical Mercy

"Endless love beyond measurement that transcends our understanding — this extravagant love pours into you until you are filled to overflowing with the fullness of God! *Never doubt* God's mighty power to work in you and accomplish all this. He will achieve infinitely more than your greatest request, your most unbelievable dream, and exceed your wildest imagination! He will outdo them all, for his miraculous power constantly energizes you."
Ephesians 3:19b-20 TPT

**Psalm 91:4, Isaiah 14:27, Psalm 32:8, 2 Peter 1:3, John 17:22, 2 Corinthians 3:18, John 8:44, Esther 4:14, 2 Corinthians 12:9, Revelation 3:7-13, Ephesians 3:14-20**

Dear one, do not fear, the end is not yet. Press in and persevere with Me: I AM. Because I AM, you are safe with Me. I cover you with My feathers, and you will not be exposed. No one can stop what I have put in motion. My gospel will be preached in all the earth. I will guide you every step as you listen to Me. Full-surrender makes Me the hand and you the glove. I am behind every movement, but the movements are seen as a glove. People will look at you and see Me. My presence already radiates from you in ways you cannot imagine. My holy presence draws hearts as you speak the truth of the gospel through your lips.

The enemy tells you lies about yourself. Stop believing him. You are amazing — you were uniquely made by Me, the Creator of all. I knit you together. He tries to send accusations to your heart that you are less than the others and the least attractive. Is he not called the father of lies? You are My delight! Today, I call you to rise up! This is My prophetic call to my people to stand up and be marked for My kingdom. An army is arising. This is an army of My faithful sons and daughters. Your faithfulness does not go unseen... it is noticed by your King. I am raising you up for a time such as this. Now is the time. I will lead your every step and the enemy will be dumbfounded. I love to shame the strong by raising up the weak in My power. My mercy will pour out through each of you to the people on the earth as a movement of the Father's love. It will shake this earth to the core in a way no one has ever seen. Radical love, radical generosity, radical mercy. Demonstrations of who I am and the simplicity and reality of My gospel. The doors are open. No man can shut them. You will receive power… as My Spirit moves through you. Your mind cannot fathom what I'm prepared to do. Fix your eyes on Me and Me alone. I am gazing at you, My child.

## Declarations and Decrees of Truth

I decree and declare that I will demonstrate radical love, generosity, and mercy.

_____

_____

_____

_____

_____

_____

_____

_____

_____

_____

_____

_____

_____

# Day 59: I Give You the Words of Life

"For where your treasure is, there your heart will be also."
Luke 12:34 NIV

**1 Corinthians 4:1, Proverbs 4:13, Psalm 119:11,
1 Corinthians 6:20, John 14:15, James 4:7, Luke 10:19,
Isaiah 55:8-9, Luke 6:38, Matthew 5:16, 1 Peter 2:9**

My child, my love is shatter-proof. I love to sit with you, here in your secret place. I give you the words of life daily. Steward them well because this pleases Me. I see that you treasure My instruction and commands. I have written My laws on your heart that you might not sin against Me. My sons and daughters must turn away from sin and fleshly desires and keep their eyes fixed on the One who gave everything for their purity. That purity was bought with a high price. Won't my children treasure it? If you love Me, you'll obey what I ask of you. Submit to Me; the devil will be resisted, and he will flee. Be confident in Me, beloved, and in My mighty ways. The enemy has been put under your feet. So as my ambassador, walk in love. This destroys his kingdom. Love in the face of hate, offer forgiveness in the face of offense, show patience in the face of persecution. My ways are higher, but I've put My Spirit in you just as I did My Son on earth. And I fill you up to overflow in order to accomplish what seems impossible to man. All things are possible in My economy. I AM. As you go, continuously walk in the way of love; let it radiate from you. I send you into darkness and dimly lit areas for the light burning within you to shine. The love and compassion spilling out of you onto My people is so beautiful. You are My ambassador of love. When you give radically, your heart imitates Mine. You are My treasured possession and I love to lavish My love and favor upon you today.

## Declarations and Decrees of Truth

I decree and declare that your WORD is a lamp to my feet and a light to my path.
I decree and declare that I will walk in purity and righteousness before the Lord.

I decree and declare that everywhere I walk, the love of Jesus will radiate from within me onto others.

_____

_____

_____

_____

_____

_____

_____

_____

_____

_____

_____

_____

_____

_____

_____

_____

_____

# Day 60: I AM a Good Father

"And since we are his true children, we qualify to share all his treasures, for indeed, we are heirs of God himself. And since we are joined to Christ, we also inherit all that he is and all that he has. We will experience being co-glorified with him provided that we accept his sufferings as our own." Romans 8:17 TPT

**Deuteronomy 10:12-13, Psalm 1:1-3, Psalm 121:5,
Song of Songs 8:6 TPT, Hebrews 4:16, Psalm 139,
Romans 5:5 TPT, Romans 12:2, James 1:22,25**

Blessed is the one who fears Me and plants himself by streams of living water. My love and My purposes for you are real. You stand at the edge of an overlook — you and I — and together we will look at the things ahead of you. Do not fear what I have dreamed of for you. Turn around and look behind you — oh, how far you've come with Me by your side. But we've only just begun, My child. I chose you. I see your obedience to My words over you, every day. For those totally committed to Me and My ways, I give big assignments. I have put fire in your heart and in your veins. Do not scrutinize My process for those around you. I use all valleys to shape My children into warriors for Me. Do you trust Me? Rest in Me, beloved. In your purity, bought by My Son, you have full access to My throne. Climb up and sit with Me. I love to speak right to your heart. I have taken notice of all your favorite things. I know you completely. Rejoice in Me! I see what this day will hold. I fill your life with good things. Share this love with all you see today. Many believe the lie that I am not a good Father. Demonstrate My love to them. I love to flow through you and show them Jesus, the hope of glory. Continue reading My Word on a continual basis. My Spirit will constantly transform you by the renewing of your mind and will empower you to walk out what truth calls you to.

## Declarations and Decrees of Truth

I decree and declare that I will demonstrate Christ's love today in tangible ways as the Holy Spirit leads me.
I decree and declare that I will abide in God's presence all through the day and feel His joy.

I decree and declare my thankfulness for belonging to the best Daddy in the world.

_____

_____

_____

_____

_____

_____

_____

_____

_____

_____

_____

_____

_____

_____

_____

_____

# Day 61: You Are a World Changer

"But you are God's chosen treasure—priests who are kings, a spiritual "nation" set apart as God's devoted ones. He called you out of darkness to experience his marvelous light, and now he claims you as his very own. He did this so that you would broadcast his glorious wonders throughout the world". 1 Peter 2:9 TPT

**Romans 10:13-15, Psalm 113:7-8, John 16:13, Zephaniah 3:17, Isaiah 41:10, Psalm 23:3, John 20:19-23, 2 Timothy 2:1 TPT, Psalm 36:5-7, Exodus 3:14, Galatians 5:24, Romans 8:5,14-17**

How beautiful are the feet of those who are carriers of My gospel! I love to empower you to share My Word and become My hands and feet. You are My courageous ambassador, My representative, My sent one. I delight in you. I sing over you, My child. Remember, My Word does not return void, but it will accomplish what I desire. My hand is upon your life. I have raised you up from the dust and lead you along My righteous path. I have led you into My truth. My breath in you has transformed you, beloved. My ways are unconventional… My ways do not fit inside human parameters. But My love for My people is fierce and unfailing. I am who I AM. I never change. But the way in which I deal with My people has changed since I sent My Son to be the spotless Lamb, who offered full atonement for your sins and the sins of the whole world. It was at this point, I adopted as children all who call upon the name of the Lord in surrender. I am tender toward My sons and daughters. My son's offering and sacrifice made you righteous in My sight. So, take this gift of righteousness seriously. Do not play around with iniquity, because it feeds the flesh. Those who live by My Spirit, cut off the fleshly desires. Fix your eyes on Jesus, look full on in His eyes, and the things of earth will grow strangely dim and unpleasing. My love is wider and deeper than the ocean. Although the journey has been difficult at times, there's a clearing ahead… do you see it? Claim, declare, and decree what I have called you to. Speak My promises, beloved… You are a WORLD-CHANGER in this generation.

## Declarations and Decrees of Truth

I decree and declare that I am a world changer, demonstrating the love of Jesus as I go.

I decree and declare that I receive power when the Holy Spirit comes upon me and I will be a witness for Jesus wherever my feet take me.

_____

_____

_____

_____

_____

_____

_____

_____

_____

_____

_____

_____

_____

_____

# Day 62: My Love Heals You

"He himself bore our sins in his body on the tree, that we might die to sin and live to righteousness. By his wounds you have been healed. For you were straying like sheep but have now returned to the Shepherd and Overseer of your souls." 1 Peter 2:24-25 ESV

Psalm 23, John 6:35, Jeremiah 33:3, Luke 4:16-21, John 14:6-10, Luke 19:10, Matthew 6:9-10, Psalm 34:18, 1 John 3:8, 1 Corinthians 15:57, Psalm 103:3-5, Job 33:4, John 10:10

Beloved, come to the table and dine with Me. Yes, I am the bread of life and I am all you need. Fall back into My arms today. I am a right-now Savior. Call to Me and I will answer you and tell you great and unsearchable things you didn't know before. My love knows no bounds. When I was on earth, I brought healing to the sick to fulfill Scripture, to show the world I was the Messiah, and to show the Father had sent me, so that mankind would know the heart of their Father: the one and only true God. I came to seek and save that which was lost and make them whole in every way. Brokenness is not found in heaven; therefore, it could not be Our will. My Father is close to the brokenhearted and He saves those crushed in spirit. Also, I came to destroy the works of darkness and shine the light of the Father's love into every dark area of sickness, disease, bondage, and strongholds. I came to bring people into the victory My Father gave me. Our love for mankind is the reason I heal the sick. If you could only fathom how great Our love is for you. I run down the mountain to the valley to meet you right where you are. I've called you by name. I am a God of healing and restoration. I pick the broken up out of the pit and set them firmly on a rock. I breathe life into their lungs and restore their lives. What the enemy came to steal and destroy, I remade better and twice as strong. Rejoice in Me, because victory is Mine and I give it to you.

## Declarations and Decrees of Truth

I decree and declare that the Lord will abundantly supply all of my needs because He is my provider.

222

I decree and declare that through intimacy with Holy Spirit, He will show me what is to come.
I decree and declare that the sick are healed by the power of Jesus Christ, when I PRAY.

# Day 63: Align Yourself with My Truth

"For if you embrace the truth, it will release true freedom into your lives." John 8:32 TPT

**Song of Songs 2:10, Ephesians 2:10, 1 Peter 5:10, 1 Peter 2:9, 2 Corinthians 6:18, Ephesians 4:24, Revelation 1:6, Isaiah 61:1-3, 1 Peter 1:7, Matthew 6:22 KJV, Isaiah 40:31**

Today, My heart sings over you. Our intimacy poses a great threat to the enemy. He will go after any place that your family's armor has a crack. But your family is Mine. The first layer of your armor is understanding your identity and value to Me. Knowing and believing I've made My sons and daughters priests and kings to be My hands and feet in the earth. You have direct access to Me — the King of all, and you have the mind of Christ through the Holy Spirit, which is living in and upon you.

Is there any way to live through difficulty and not learn how to walk through the fire? Experience is an excellent teacher. I am a God of restoration and I will use the ashes to make beauty. I will turn the fire that he tried to destroy you with, into a tool of refinement and purification. As you fully align with My Word, My truth, and My heart, you will become someone that I break chains through. People who were in similar bondage will hear your testimony coupled with the TRUTH and get free. Chains fall off when the lies no longer have anywhere to hold onto because you believe My Word. Holiness is My way for you. Fix your single eye on Me, your Father, who loves you and gave everything for you. I desire full communion. Connect your thoughts with Me all through your day, and I will tell you secrets. I will guide you as you walk, and you will not stumble. Those who hope in the Lord will renew their strength, you will soar on My wings like eagles, seeing your world from My perspective. I will give you My eyes for the path you are walking. My eyes of love are for every person you meet. Lies are crushed and have nowhere to land in a heart that is fully connected to Mine. I have always loved you every moment of your life. There has never been a moment that I wasn't waiting on you to come back to Me with understanding of My love. I have created you to be amazing in so many ways, My child. I have so much to tell you. Bring your ear to Me. I will confirm you are hearing Me, as you believe Me over the lies trying to gain entrance to your mind. All that I call you to do, I empower you to complete. Come to Me and rest in Me. Sit with Me and we will talk about many things I have put in your heart. I have created you for My love.

### Declarations and Decrees of Truth

I decree and declare that I have the shield of faith and every fiery arrow is extinguished.

_____

_____

_____

_____

_____

_____

_____

_____

_____

_____

_____

_____

# Day 64: Rest in My Shadow

"He who dwells in the secret place of the Most High, shall abide under the shadow of the Almighty. I will say of the LORD, "He is my refuge and my fortress; My God, in Him I will trust." Psalms 91:1-2 NKJV

**Psalm 23:6, Hebrews 4:12-13, 1 John 2:1-2, Ephesians 5:26-27, Romans 5:1-5, Ephesians 1:3-14, Psalm 46:10 NASB, 2 Timothy 2:25-26 NLT, Psalm 36:5-7**

Beloved child, you are mine. I sit with you in your secret place and I follow you all the days of your life. I see your heart and your intentions. If you fall into sin, come back to Me quickly, in repentance, and receive My forgiveness. You are a washed, purified vessel. Stand tall, knowing My favor is upon you. As you walk with Me, I strengthen your character. I care about the hearts of My children. I love to come alongside My kids during trials and storms, building your trust and teaching you who you are in Me. Many of My children don't understand son-ship. They believe they must work and strive for this. The enemy has told them lies and twisted My gospel. This thing is simple. I came to rescue and set free. You receive son-ship at salvation and then live in radical surrender from the place of being My beloved. You must fix your eyes on Me and walk in step with Me. Don't focus on others; focus on Me. We walk on an unfamiliar path... unfamiliar to the world. Give Me more of your ear. Press in. Seek Me and rest in my shadow. There is no striving. Tell those around you about My unfailing love.

## Declarations and Decrees of Truth

I decree and declare that (put in their name) understands their son-ship and identity in Christ.

I decree and declare that all lies of fear and anxiety are crushed in their lives.

I decree and declare that I do not have to check off a list or strive to be loved and favored by God, because I am His precious beloved child (at my salvation).

# Day 65: Stand Up in My Waves of Mercy

"Yet hope returns when I remember this one thing:
The Lord's unfailing love and mercy still continue,
fresh as the morning, as sure as the sunrise. The
Lord is all I have, and so in him I put my hope."
Lamentations 3:21-24 GNT

**John 14:17, Mark 16:17-18, Psalm 86:15, 2 Corinthians 3:17, Jeremiah 30:17, Matthew 9:35-36, Matthew 10:1, 1 Corinthians 15:57, John 14:12, Revelation 12:10-11, Psalm 1:2-3, Daniel 2:26-28 NLT**

Beloved one, I see how the sun rises and sets on every one of your days. My presence hovers near you constantly. Your life is very important to Me. I've created you for a time such as this. Those who surrender to the Lord their God will see signs and wonders as they share My gospel. Signs and wonders will become the norm, not the exception. Stand confidently in My authority I give you. You are Mine and My love for you is unfailing, complete, and unconditional. Stand up in My waves of mercy. You never walk alone. The best is yet to come! Where My Spirit is, there is freedom. Freedom from darkness, oppression, and hopelessness. Surrender to Me daily. As you surrender, We will breathe life into those in your path who are desperate. Love them. Ask them if they know Me.

Trust Me fully. It is I who heals… I will flow through you like rivers of living water. Hold your faith up, my child. I still raise the dead! Also, I raise dead hopes to life and reveal who I am. I give you authority over all sickness and disease. Nothing is too hard for Me, so stand in My victory. Fix your eyes on Me and just watch what I will do. Expect miracles—greater ones. In order to see greater ones, we go deeper, farther away from the safety of the boat. The wind of My Spirit will catch more and more people ablaze. We stand in victory together in these last days. Satan is defeated along with his lies. Walk closely with Me and listen as I pour My truth into your mind. More beloved… read My Word more. Meditate on it day and night. I will show you mysteries in My Word and reveal secrets that will astound you.

## Declarations and Decrees of Truth

I decree and declare that I am chosen by God to do the good works He prepared in advance for me to do.

I decree and declare that I am empowered supernaturally by the Holy Spirit to be a witness to others of the goodness of God.

_____

_____

_____

_____

_____

_____

_____

_____

_____

_____

_____

_____

_____

_____

_____

_____

# Day 66: The Greatest Awakening Ever

"Arise, shine, for your light has come, and the glory of the Lord has risen upon you. For behold, darkness shall cover the earth, and thick darkness the peoples; but the Lord will arise upon you, and his glory will be seen upon you. And nations shall come to your light, and kings to the brightness of your rising." Isaiah 60:1-3 ESV

**Philippians 4:6-8 TPT, 1 Corinthians 13:1-7, Matthew 6:33-34, Deuteronomy 30:19-20, 1 Corinthians 14:1, Acts 2:17-21, Hebrews 12:2, Hebrews 11:1, 6, James 1:22-24, Matthew 24:14**

Dear beloved, I love to demonstrate my love to My children. Sometimes, when you feel My presence in your daily activities, that is Me drawing near you and confirming My ways. Because I'm holding onto you with My great love, you can run hard after Me and My kingdom. Do not be tempted to feel overwhelmed. I am faithful to help you—simply take one day at a time. Determine to take care of that day's business or accomplish one thing a day. If you aren't successful, do not heap guilt on yourself. Instead, thank Me for all we did do, and start fresh the next day. Don't let lists run your life or steal your joy. Live your life, in love, to the fullest measure. People matter more than things. Love everyone you pass by. I will radiate My presence all around you. It's My presence that takes man's breath away, but I love to draw near to them through My humble vessels like you. Are you willing to speak My heart to people that you meet?

I am creating a deeper hunger in your heart for prophecy. Healing pertains to some, but prophecy pertains to all. My heart has gifts of My love to give every person. For some, it will plant seeds, for others it will bring increase and salvation. My Holy Spirit is being poured out onto my people in measures you've never experienced before. I want you to be sensitive to My voice, no matter where you are: home, car, store, school, or wherever you find yourself. I am moving and all who call upon My name will be saved. The enemy has been defeated. Although, in the past, it has looked as if he was winning on earth, but no longer. The coming harvest will be the greatest awakening the earth has ever seen. Just keep your eyes open and fixed on Me, the author and perfecter of your faith. I will use those who are earnestly seeking Me in astounding ways. The supernatural lifestyle follows those who are willing to follow Me, in faith, rather than what they see immediately in the natural. Those who put their faith into action show me the extent of their faith. The disciples didn't just tell people about Me, they proved their faith in Me with their lives. I was there, with them, in life. Nothing has changed. I still have followers... some are only talkers, and some show Me their faith by stepping into risk. I am with you every step of the way. Be a continual listener. You never go alone. Together, we will turn this world upside down!

### Declarations and Decrees of Truth

I decree and declare that will see multitudes saved in Jesus' name.

_____

_____

_____

_____

_____

_____

_____

_____

_____

_____

# Day 67: Do You Trust Me?

"Those who know your name trust in you, for you,
Lord, have never forsaken those who seek you."
Psalm 9:10 NIV

**1 John 5:14, Isaiah 41:10, Hebrews 4:13, Matthew 7:9, Psalm 37:23,
Psalm 25:12, Matthew 10:29, Isaiah 55:2-3, James 1:5, Romans 4:17,
Job 22:28 NASB, Proverbs 18:21, Colossians 3:15, Matthew 6:33,
Romans 5:5, 1 Corinthians 15:58**

I am here, listening to every word you bring to Me, written and spoken. My plans for you are great. Do you trust Me? Do not fear, for I am with you, do not be dismayed or worried, for I am your God. I will strengthen you and help you and I will uphold you with My right hand. I have plenty of resources… I created the whole world. Do I not know every heart? Would I give you a stone instead of bread? You say I'm a good Father, yet do you believe it? Look at Me, My child, I am gazing at you with eyes of love. I have this world in My hands, and I order every step of the righteous who fear Me. I see every sparrow that falls to the ground. I know every detail of every heart. You and your family are mine. Do not fear the situations that arise. Do not listen to your eyes and ears when faced with fear... instead listen to My voice. I am here to guide you along the path unseen. My love will guard you. My protection is over you. Reject fear and intimidation. You are my brave ambassador of love, and I breathe life into your very being. My wisdom in every situation is, indeed, what you need.

When you hunger to know Me, it does not go unnoticed. Stand firm on My promises. Stand firm on My faithfulness. Decree what I will do. Speak out My will as you hear it. Call into being that which is not yet. Create My purposes with your words. Speak healing as I show you. When you speak peace, envision it. Believe your words are becoming reality. I have put the power of life or death in the tongue, so speak life and expect it. This is what I did, beloved. This is faith. Seek first the kingdom and all these things will be added to you as you obey. Become love as you go. I AM hope and I shine through you.

## Declarations and Decrees of Truth

I decree and declare that fear is far from me because I am drenched in the LOVE of God and His love casts out my fear. I decree and declare that I will speak the promises of God until they come to pass.

_____

_____

_____

_____

_____

_____

_____

_____

_____

_____

_____

_____

_____

_____

_____

# Day 68: I AM the Master Painter

"For we are God's masterpiece. He has created us
anew in Christ Jesus, so we can do the good things he
planned for us long ago." Ephesians 2:10 NLT

**2 Corinthians 2:14, Ephesians 5:1-2, Haggai 2:9, 2 Corinthians 3:18,
Isaiah 43:18-19, Ephesians 1:3-11, 1 Peter 1:6-7, James 1:22, Luke 11:28**

My child, you are so pleasing to My heart. I have so much to paint on the canvas of your life. The colors I see over you are breathtaking. The fragrance is tantalizing to Me because your desire is to please Me, not man. I've switched mediums for this next painting and I'm upgrading My paint. This next painting will have My glory woven into every stroke. Wait till you begin to see what I am planning to paint this time over your life. It's even more beautiful than the first one. Not that I have discarded the beautiful former painting, it's lovely. But, see I am doing a new thing. Look at your artist… your Creator. I will show you the way to step. With every glorious brush-stroke, we will create something beautiful that will help usher in My kingdom to earth. With every work of art, there is a specific process. I have dreamed about you and your life from the foundation of the world. I am the Master Painter. And I am the one who turns barriers into blessings. Just wait! There is much goodness in the days ahead. I strengthen you in the fires of My love. Purity of heart from the heat of trials has made you stronger and is teaching you who you are in Me. I am transferring the knowledge of your identity from your head to your heart. This is where a shift occurs in My sons and daughters. You actually "become My word" in this place… like Jesus.

## Declarations and Decrees of Truth

I decree and declare that I arise and shine because Jesus, the light in me, has come and the glory of the Lord has risen upon me. I decree and declare that Christ is leading me in His triumphal procession, and through me spreads the fragrance of the knowledge of Him every place I go.
I decree and declare that I am (or your loved one's name here) a beautiful masterpiece in the hands of the Father.

# Day 69: Come Stand Near the Flame of My Spirit

"Since we are receiving our rights to an unshakeable Kingdom, we should be extremely thankful and offer God the purest worship that delights his heart as we lay down our lives in absolute surrender, filled with awe. For our God is a holy, devouring fire!" Hebrews 12:28-29 TPT

**Isaiah 43:1-5, Hosea 10:12, Galatians 5:1, Luke 4:18, 2 Timothy 2:19-21, Psalm 25:9, Matthew 11:28, 1 Corinthians 15:58, Exodus 14:14, John 6:63, John 14:26, 1 John 4:4, Hebrews 12:2, 1 John 5:19**

A flame in front of you to lead your way step-by-step, and a fire behind you to keep you burning with my passion… this is the way the servants of the Lord will walk in these last days. I have called you by name, you are Mine. My love is like a soaking rain, penetrating through the outer layers of your being, straight to your soul. Day after day, I speak My glorious hope to your mind, will, and emotions. I am moving you into freedom. Give Me your attention as we move together. I love to be near you. Nothing is wasted: walking in the depths teaches you to look up and focus on Me… soaring on the heights tests your humility. I am creating a vessel that can STAND on My Word, despite pressure and weight from the world. You will become a vessel I can trust with My glory and power, one that trusts in Me, no matter what your eyes see. I hear your every desire. Come to Me and I will give you rest. Exhaustion comes from the world, but true refreshment is from standing near the flame of My Spirit.

You are becoming firm and steadfast, My child. My love is turning your heart fully toward Me, knowing I will fight for you. I am your defender and your protector. I AM. I *still* am I AM. Blessed is the one who humbles himself for the sake of following Me in obedience. I draw near to you through My Spirit. My words are spirit and they are life. Freedom belongs to those who trust in Me to set them free. I am greater than the one in the world and I am in you. Fix your eyes on the One you trust. Don't look and stare at the problem or the situation. Look at your Defender, your Deliverer, your Savior… who saves you from sin, sickness, and the wicked one.

## Declarations and Decrees of Truth

I decree and declare that I recognize lies from the enemy in the battlefield of my mind, take them captive, and make them obedient to the truth of the WORD.

I decree and declare that when I know the truth, the truth will set me free.

# Day 70: Open Your Eyes to My Plans of Wonder

"I keep asking that the God of our Lord Jesus Christ, the glorious Father, may give you the Spirit of wisdom and revelation, so that you may know him better. I pray that the eyes of your heart may be enlightened in order that you may know the hope to which he has called you, the riches of his glorious inheritance in his holy people, and his incomparably great power for us who believe."
Ephesians 1:17-19a NIV

**Zephaniah 3:17, Psalm 91:1-4, 1 Corinthians 14:33, Matthew 5:14, 2 Peter 1:4, 2 Timothy 3:5 NLT, Romans 8:17, Proverbs 25:2, John 16:12, Isaiah 43:18-19, Song of Songs 7:1-9 TPT**

Beloved child, my heart delights in you. Come close to Me in our time together this day. I want to whisper My love to you. Whispers come to those who stay in close proximity to each other. Come closer. Come sit with Me in my shadow. I will shelter you from the difficulties that come your way, ones that you don't even know about. In My shadow, you hear My whispers of truth that keep you focused and on My path of righteousness. My voice also leads you in the right direction, with My revelation light shining and cutting through the darkness. You'll never be lost or confused if you consciously stay connected to Me, My child. My loving arms hold you today. Do you perceive this? Open the eyes of your heart wide to Me. Secrets are revealed to those who have eyes to see.

My love radiates from you to those in need. Let it flow! Be the light, My beloved one. You are a partaker in My divine nature. I see the wrestling that occurs in your heart to make sure you are walking in truth. The enemy wants to twist and push My sons and daughters off the path of authority and power... back into the weak mindset that's prevailed for centuries. But I am revealing My Word and the truth therein. Attach yourself to your source and allow Me to reveal revelation truth, so that you can not only step into your destiny, but also teach others their identities as well. As My adopted children, you are royalty. There are many things being revealed now that have been concealed in My Word. My Spirit reveals My truth as you can bear its weight. Look at Me and get ready to learn more. I am rushing in, onto the scene of planet earth, and blessed is the one who fully surrenders to the new thing I am doing... My plans of wonder.

## Declarations and Decrees of Truth

I decree and declare that the love of God in my life will draw people to Jesus.

I decree and declare that I am the object of the Lord's deepest love and affection.

_____

_____

_____

_____

_____

_____

_____

_____

_____

_____

_____

_____

_____

# Day 71: Just Surrender to Me

"My old self has been crucified with Christ. It is no longer I who live, but Christ lives in me. So I live in this earthly body by trusting in the Son of God, who loved me and gave himself for me." Galatians 2:20 NLT

**Acts 3:19, 1 John 4:16-19, Luke 12:11-12, John 16:13, Joshua 1:9, 1 John 5:4, Romans 11:29 John 15:4 TPT, Psalm 139:1-5, Song of Songs 4:8-9**

My love covers you, My child. I am working behind the scenes for you. Trust in Me and My words. Continue in obedience each day. When you fail, repent and run back to My arms. I am waiting to embrace you—every time! My love casts away fear. Fear will not even come near you. Come closer to this contagious flame of My love. I will breathe on your heart and soul and set you ablaze to a new level. My ways are higher. Come higher with Me. Like a toddler keeps his eyes on his parents as he toddles across the floor, likewise, keep your eyes fixed on Me as you walk through life, knowing that I'll pick you up when you fall down. You belong to Me and I'm so proud of you. You bring me such joy. You don't have to fit into a mold that looks like other people's callings or gifts. Explore and surrender to who I've created YOU to become. Ask Me. When you're at the base of a mountain in your life, and you're looking up, don't worry if it's blocking your way. Look at Me and move in step with Me as I teach you what to say and do, in the moment. Turn your affection toward Me in your thoughts. My Spirit is in you to guide you. You are never alone. NEVER. You can't fail because I have already won the victory for you. I will help you get there if you surrender and give Me the reins. Just let go of your control, My child. Close your eyes and come up here and I'll show you where we are going, from My heavenly perspective. Fellowshipping with Me in full communion sets the rhythm of our journey. Our movement is determined by your surrender. Fall backwards into My hands and see… I'll catch you. My precious child, I know where you're going to step, and the thoughts that propel you that way before one of them comes to mind. Come snuggle with Me in reckless abandon and watch Me catapult you forward into your destiny. I AM still.

## Declarations and Decrees of Truth

I decree and declare that today I yield my life to you, oh God. I fall back into your arms.
I decree and declare that I will live as an original and not a copy of someone else.

_____

_____

_____

_____

_____

_____

_____

_____

_____

_____

_____

_____

_____

_____

_____

_____

# Day 72: Who Will Reach Them?

"Then the King will say to those on his right, 'Come, you who are blessed by my Father, inherit the Kingdom prepared for you from the creation of the world. For I was hungry, and you fed me. I was thirsty, and you gave me a drink. I was a stranger, and you invited me into your home. I was naked, and you gave me clothing. I was sick, and you cared for me. I was in prison, and you visited me.' "Then these righteous ones will reply, 'Lord, when did we ever see you hungry and feed you? Or thirsty and give you something to drink? Or a stranger and show you hospitality? Or naked and give you clothing? When did we ever see you sick or in prison and visit you?' "And the King will say, 'I tell you the truth, when you did it to one of the least of these my brothers and sisters, you were doing it to me!'" Matthew 25:34-40 NLT

**John 1:48, Luke 18:1-8, Jeremiah 29:12-14, James 2:15-16, Luke 4:18-19, 1 John 3:16, Matthew 18:12, 1 John 4:12, Luke 14:12-14, Psalm 12:5, Proverbs 22:9**

My child, I see you. I know you. I created you for a time such as this. Some days, there is a war against our time in the secret place, but you will be victorious to find Me daily when you pray and don't give up. I am always near to you, and I will be found by you, beloved. My love surrounds you today... do you perceive it? I am giving you a piece of My heart for the unvalued. The poor of the earth have my attention—just as an earthly father is concerned when his children have nothing to eat, how much more am I concerned with My hungry ones? My love and care race to meet the needs of the desolate, broken, and abandoned. I want you to value those I value. All human life is valuable. Jesus' life was laid down for every person. Who will reach them? Who will give a cup of water to My desperate ones calling out to Me? Who will help those starving, with nowhere to lay their head? I stop for the one. That one is so valuable to Me. In order for my children to know My heart for people, they must know Me. I love the way you tune your ears to hear My voice. Move forward with Me. Open your eyes to love people as you go. This is how I did it, noticing the least of these to society. Keep in sync with My heart, and do not entertain condemnation from the enemy. As with many things in your life, he desires to slow you down to eventual derailment. But with your eyes fixed on Me, finally believing the truth about who you are — you change the world — for the ONE. I am the Author and Finisher of your faith. I will never leave you or forsake you. You are Mine.

## Declarations and Decrees of Truth

I decree and declare that I will open my eyes to see the needs of your people, GIVE generously, and show them love.

_____

_____

_____

_____

_____

_____

_____

_____

_____

_____

_____

_____

# Day 73: Testify of My Love

"But the man who had been set free begged Jesus over and over not to leave, saying, "Let me be with you!" Jesus sent him away with these instructions: "Return to your home and your family and tell them all the wonderful things God has done for you." So the man went away and preached to everyone who would listen about the amazing miracle Jesus had worked in his life." Luke 8:38-39 TPT

**Exodus 19:5, Psalm 103:13-17, 2 Timothy 1:7,**
**Acts 1:8, Psalm 34, Ephesians 2:10, 1 John 2:6,**
**2 Corinthians 3:18 TPT, Songs of Songs 7:1 TPT**

Beloved, you are my precious treasured possession. My heart is connected to yours and this is why you feel such compassion for people. There are so many I want to reach through you. Break agreement with the spirit of fear and the fear of what man thinks. Align yourself with My Word. I haven't given you hesitation. I've given you My love, power, and a sound mind. Live in My love and be yourself. When you step out and risk to show love to someone, I will show My power through your simple obedience to love and pray for those I highlight to you. If you find yourself in a conversation with someone, go with it. Tell them of My love and how My love has changed your life. *Testify*. Let My joy be on the edge of your tongue and in your smile. I see obedience, not "success." When your feelings don't line up — praise Me, anyway. In your obedience, I will push the lies aside, so My joy will shine through. You are My ambassador of love. Do not let the enemy hinder who I've created you to be. You are who I say you are. You are Mine. I adore you — every part of you. Even though you see parts of yourself that you do not believe are desirable, I love all of you. I created you. You are my magnum opus… that's right, the pinnacle of My creation. All my kids are. Not all of them have come into this understanding or see themselves as one of My masterpieces. But I am shaping all My sons and daughters into the image of My Son with all their own unique qualities.

## Declarations and Decrees of Truth

I decree and declare that God's supernatural love radiates from me to the one I stop to talk to and pray for.

I decree and declare that my family and I are covered by the blood of Jesus and his banner over us is love. No weapon formed against us will prosper.

_____

_____

_____

_____

_____

_____

_____

_____

_____

_____

_____

_____

_____

_____

_____

_____

# Day 74: If You Don't Quit, You Win

"So you must remain in life-union with me, for I remain in life-union with you. For as a branch severed from the vine will not bear fruit, so your life will be fruitless unless you live your life intimately joined to mine." John 15:4 TPT

**John 17:3, Matthew 9:13, 2 Chronicles 16:9a, Psalm 63, 1 Samuel 15:10-23, Romans 8:1-9, Romans 13:14**

My dear child, blessed are you when you delight in My ways and want to know My heart. Great is the reward of those who earnestly seek me unselfishly, instead of personal gain. I see the difference. A relationship with Me goes both ways... I want for you to tell Me everything in your heart, but I have much to tell you about Mine, if you only ask. Many people hear that Christianity is a relationship, but do not think our relationship could be as close and meaningful as human relationships. That is proof they don't know Me. I love intimacy with My family. Intimacy is based on mutual closeness and love. I wait to see who will come near to Me, desiring Me instead of their eyes focusing on personal gain. David sought me for intimacy; Saul for what I could give him. I will give you the key of David's intimacy with Me: a life laid down to our love and friendship, knowing I am fully able to do more than you could ask or imagine, according to the power at work within you. Nothing is impossible for My lovers who believe Me, who are determined to DO MY WILL, and carry out My plans. Walking in love with the fear of the Lord, balanced with intimacy with My heart, will prove to be the most incredibly powerful place to be in this hour.

THOSE WHO CAN HEAR MY VOICE AND DO WHAT I SAY will walk around every wall and trap set by the enemy. Nothing will stop my SENT ONES. So practice this, beloved. Practice hearing Me in every decision. I am waiting on you to involve Me in your resolutions. Most are made at the discretion of your flesh, or the growling of your stomach. Pull back the reins of your flesh leading you. Ask Me. Act on what you hear or perceive. Be diligent. If you act on something and it seems to be non-productive, keep going. Try again. This is how you learn and perfect the leading of My Spirit. You've had many successes in this, but work toward being led in every moment. This is My will for you. Remember in Acts, when my sons said, "It seemed good to the Holy Spirit and to us…" (Acts 15:28). Ask the Spirit. The more you surrender your will to Mine, the more you will hear. One more thing… this kind of obedience scares the enemy to death. He will throw distraction, doubt, and blockades your way, but keep going. If you don't quit, you win. Come closer to Me and be unified with Me and My plans through full communion.

### Declarations and Decrees of Truth:

I decree and declare that I will live connected to the Holy Spirit and DO WHAT HE SHOWS ME TO DO.

# Day 75: You are a Chosen Remnant

"And that is but one example of what God is doing in
this age of fulfillment, for God's grace empowers his
chosen remnant. And since it is by God's grace, it can't
be a matter of their good works; otherwise, it wouldn't
be a gift of grace, but earned by human effort."
Romans 11:5-6 TPT

**1 Corinthians 13, John 7:37-38, Psalm 57:10, Psalm 37:4,
Jeremiah 1:12, Jeremiah 32:17, Romans 3:24, Matthew 17:20**

Dear one to my heart… love. Practice love today. This is
on my heart, because many do not know what it means to be
loved, nor do they know MY LOVE. As John 7 explains, love
the one before you with My rivers of living water. I am flowing
through you, as my vessel. Never underestimate the power of
my love. My love for you stretches beyond the heavens into
eternity. I have beautiful dreams for you… As you lay down
earthly things to take up My will for you, they will become
manifest in your life. My dreams are bigger than yours, and
I can see the dreams in your heart. In the waiting, praise Me
for what is to come. I am not slow in keeping My promises to
you, I have a perfect Chronos and Kairos time in mind. Your
trust in My hand on your life gets my attention. Keep going.
Do what I've given you and do not forsake prayer. I think I've
made Myself abundantly clear that prayer does, indeed, shift
realities. Call into being My promises of destiny and healing.
Nothing is too hard or too big for Me, your Source.

I AM. I've not changed since Moses' day. But, because of
my covenant fulfilled through Jesus, you are made right with
Me and can come into My presence. Therefore, you are able to
bask in My love and kindness and grace. You were created to
walk with Me in intimacy for the escalation of My end-time
harvest season. All things will be possible for My laid-down
lovers, who fully believe Me for astounding miracles, signs,
and wonders. You are in a special remnant for a time such as
this. I chose you.

## Declarations and Decrees of Truth

I decree and declare that my family and I are kept from falling and presented blameless before the presence of God with great joy… to GOD be the glory. (Jude 24)

I decree and declare that sickness, disease, oppression, possession, and demonic attack are under my feet when I take authority in Christ. (Luke 10:19)

_____

_____

_____

_____

_____

_____

_____

_____

_____

_____

_____

_____

_____

_____

# Day 76: I Desire
## Wholeness for All

"*You know of* Jesus of Nazareth, how God anointed Him with the Holy Spirit and with power, and *how* He went about doing good and **healing all** who were oppressed by the devil, for God was with Him." Acts 10:38 NASB

**Isaiah 66:2, Proverbs 30:5, 1 Corinthians 2:13, Isaiah 26:3, Psalm 84:11, John 16:13, Proverbs 8:17**

Dearly beloved, My will is to see healing for your whole family. I have paid the price. You don't have to fight alone… I am with you. Line up your desires with Mine: My love for humanity is great and I desire wholeness for all. How could My desire be sickness and death? I am LOVE. I gave My life so you could live. The traditions of men are deeply ingrained into the thinking in My church… but I am breaking the chains in the hearts of My sons and daughters. Those whose hearts are humble and contrite before Me will have their eyes opened. Blessed is He whose heart is humble and teachable, who trembles at My Word. The Word of God is pure, but some of the interpretation has been corrupted over time. As you read the Word, ask me for the interpretation for each scripture verse. I am Faithful, I am your Counselor, your Guide, your Interpreter, your Friend, your Lover, your Savior, and your Partner in this life. Turn to Me in every situation. I am one thought away from conversation and intimacy. But I will wait on you… I must see your commitment and desire for abiding with Me. I am leading you into all truth. No good thing will I withhold from you or from those whose walk is blameless. Commit your way to Me and I will give you the desires of your heart—which will align with My desires. I love you, child. You are My beloved one, whom I treasure. I formed you and created you uniquely for such a time as this. Seek Me with all of your heart and do not forsake our intimacy. Listening to Me will be your lifeline for truth and miracles. I adore you and I continue to gaze at you with eyes of love.

## Declarations and Decrees of Truth

I decree and declare that I give mercy, grace, and forgiveness to others, even the undeserving.

I decree and declare that I am blessed by the Lord and in every area of my life, I surrender.

---

# DAY 77: THE BLIND WILL SEE

"I, the Lord, have called You in righteousness, and will hold
Your hand; I will keep You and give You as a covenant to
the people, as a light to the Gentiles, to open **blind** eyes, to
bring out prisoners from the prison, those who sit in darkness from the prison house... I will bring the **blind** by a
way they did not know; I will lead them in paths they have
not known. I will make darkness light before them, and
crooked places straight. These things I will do for them,
and not forsake them." Isaiah 42:6-7,16 NKJV

**Ephesians 5:1-2, Mark 16:18-19, John 10:27, Isaiah 42,**
**Mark 7:5-13, 2 Peter 3:9, Psalm 138:1-3**

Beloved, I treasure you. I want closeness between us. Tell
Me the things on your heart and I will tell you what's on
Mine. In obedience, walk with Me in love everywhere you
go. Together, we will pray for the sick, the captive, and you
will experience signs and wonders. There is an expectation
of surety, just as you know that when you turn your affection toward Me, I will speak. As you expect it with no doubts,
YOU HEAR ME. This is the same amount of faith and surety
to see the life I've given YOU—flow into other people. Believe
My Word more than what your eyes see. This is why I call my
people "blind" in Isaiah 42. They are blind to being able to
firmly believe My promises until the reality comes into their
sight. Their ears are deaf because they hear My Word, but do
not believe it for what it says. They hold to what traditions of
men have taught My Word to mean. I want to open your beautiful eyes to My truth about healing. It is my desire for every
person to be healed, but ultimately, I want salvation for their
lost and wandering souls. I do not wish any to perish, but all
to come to repentance. This is my way for you: tell them My
good news. Who will go if not My own, beloved children? The
ones I've given my life for. Who I call, I equip.

I am faithful to complete the work I began in you. Continue
in your trust in Me. Keep in step with My Spirit. The path may
be unfamiliar to you, but not to Me. I am the one who gives
breath and life to those who turn to Me. The more you seek

Me, the closer we become, My child. My presence is already with you and in you but will increase—flowing out of you as our intimacy increases. Surrendered hearts are those who "see." Submit yourself in entirety to My will and, together, we will open blind eyes, free captives, and release many from the dungeons of the enemy. They will see the goodness of the Lord. Believe My Word above your eyesight. I am the Lord and My Word is truth and it will stand. I have exalted My Word above My own name. Declare My Word over your life and do not back down. Watch what happens. I love you.

## Declarations and Decrees of Truth

I decree and declare as I yield to the Spirit, I will speak His truth in a way the blind see and the deaf hear. They will be set free by the Spirit of the Lord.

# Day 78: Let Go of Your Offense and Forgive

"Since God chose you to be the holy people he loves, you must clothe yourselves with tenderhearted mercy, kindness, humility, gentleness, and patience. Make allowance for each other's faults and forgive anyone who offends you. Remember, the Lord forgave you, so you must forgive others. For love is supreme and must flow through each of these virtues. Love becomes the mark of true maturity." Colossians 3:12-14 TPT

**Matthew 11:28, Isaiah 53:3-5, Matthew 5:6, John 3:34 TPT, John 7:37-38, Proverbs 2:6, Matthew 24:14, 1 Peter 2:9**

My beloved one, come to me with your burdens. All of them. Let go of your offense and forgive. Love, despite being wronged. Fix your eyes on Me: I paid for all your iniquities. I did not do anything in My life to deserve it, yet I took all sin, iniquities, and wrongs upon Myself. Though unfair by earthly standards, my love covered it all. Sometimes, you'll be asked to bear things that aren't your fault, without offense. Bear the burden with love and humility. This will point people back to Me. Let go of your "fear of man." Fear ME only. Stop worrying about your reputation and follow Me. How others view you comes second to My view of you. This life will be unjust, especially for My followers. But your reward is beyond your imagination, and I am with your reward. I love you.

I see the hunger in your heart. Blessed are those who hunger and thirst after righteousness for they will be filled… and you shall be filled to overflow without measure. This overflow of My Spirit will change the world around you. It will be a torrent of living water, rushing from your belly, My child. Continue in communion with Me, moment by moment. Listen to My voice in every circumstance, because I will give you divine wisdom and direction. There will be many, many, many saved before I return for my treasured bride—many who think they're Christians will be saved and will surrender all to Me. Brace yourself for My intense love to flow through you in these last days. This is your destiny. I call My sons and daughters to lead people out of the darkness into My marvelous light.

## Declarations and Decrees of Truth

I decree and declare that I fear God, and not man, so I will walk in daily forgiveness and not pick up offense toward others.
I decree and declare that I am a conduit of the intense LOVE of the Father to flow through everywhere I go.

_____

_____

_____

_____

_____

_____

_____

_____

_____

_____

_____

_____

_____

_____

# Day 79: Love Even When Others Curse

Jesus said, "Your ancestors have also been taught 'Love your neighbors and hate the one who hates you.' However, I say to you, love your enemy, bless the one who curses you, do something wonderful for the one who hates you, and respond to the very ones who persecute you by praying for them. For that will reveal your identity as children of your heavenly Father. He is kind to all by bringing the sunrise to warm and rainfall to refresh whether a person does what is good or evil." Matthew 5:43-45 TPT

**Matthew 5:43-48, Proverbs 23:26, Psalm 103:10, Luke 6:30-35, Romans 2:4, Psalm 84:11, 1 Peter 1:15-16, Revelation 7:9-10, Isaiah 61:10, Ephesians 4:2, Romans 12:1, 1 John 3:16**

My child, you belong to Me. I think you're beginning to see that the calling on your life is not ordinary or powerless. Your sonship is supernatural. I have heard your prayers for your loved one. Do not fear, I am faithful. Remember not to let sin *against* you produce sin *within* you. Just as I don't treat you as your sins deserve, so you must give grace to others. The fear of the Lord causes you to love when others curse. Bless them, especially when they're mad at you. This is not a natural human function, but My Spirit lives in you. Serve them. Love is a sacrifice. Love them the way they need to be loved. Pray for them to see their true identity in Me. Do not treat them the way they treat you… treat them the way you'd like to be treated: with kindness, respect, and mercy. My goodness and mercy lead people to repentance. Trust me, beloved, I love them more than you do. Ask Me for extra grace and lavish it upon them. It is My good pleasure to provide for My precious children. This is My desire and My will. Keep your eyes on Me. No good thing will I withhold from he whose walk is blameless. Walk in holiness. Be holy, as I am holy. You are robed in white before Me, because Jesus has paid for your righteousness. Keep your eyes on me and live in humility beloved… and in surrender. Total surrender is where life really begins. This is where life in the natural gives way to the supernatural life. So, go and love them well and show them My love… My unconditional love.

## Declarations and Decrees of Truth

I decree and declare that God's love flowing through me, will stop the enemy's schemes of division and hatred in its tracks. I decree and declare that I will offer myself as a living sacrifice today and allow the Holy Spirit to give me words of blessing for those undeserving.

_____

_____

_____

_____

_____

_____

_____

_____

_____

_____

_____

_____

_____

# Day 80: Go Deeper with Me

"So above all, guard the affections of your heart, for they affect all that you are. Pay attention to the welfare of your innermost being, for from there flows the wellspring of life."
Proverbs 4:23 TPT

**1 Corinthians 2:9-11, Matthew 25:14-30, Proverbs 3:5, Hebrews 11:1,6, Romans 10:17, 2 Corinthians 5:7, Romans 14:17, Psalm 42:7 TPT, Matthew 11:29, Matthew 17:20, Matthew 14:29, Matthew 7:7, Mark 16:18-19, Psalm 81:10**

Step deeper into risk, beloved. My hand is with you, guiding you on your way. I am aligning your heart with Mine. The Holy Spirit covers you with righteousness, peace, and joy. Go deeper with me and meditate on My Word. Speak it and declare it over your family. It will come to pass. Deep calls to deep… I will give you prophetic words for My beloved children who need to hear My heart. Honor Me by speaking what you hear. My voice is gentle and humble in heart. I am the same now as I was when I walked on earth—I never change. My love, compassion, and desire for healing remains steadfast. I love you. I impart to you power and authority in the spiritual realm. Remember, faith is not a feeling. Act upon it and then the mountain will move, not before. Take a step on the water, then you can walk. Risk in the natural realm is faith in the spiritual realm. When in doubt about what to do, ask Me. My Spirit loves to guide and direct you and He is faithful, My child.

There is coming an outpouring of My Spirit upon My people like nothing you've ever seen. It will come up from the wellspring of your heart, and the river of the spirit within you will begin to overflow its banks. Everywhere you go, My Spirit will touch people with the power of the living God. There will be signs and wonders, and I will confirm My Word as you speak it. Open your mouth, and I will fill it, as I did with Peter, Paul, and Stephen. The more you live surrendered to My purposes, the more I will use you in greater measure. Let go and fall into My mighty arms. I will never leave you. I am faithful, My child. You are a treasure to Me.

## Declarations and Decrees of Truth

I decree and declare that as for me and my family, WE WILL SERVE THE LORD.

I decree and declare that God will fill my mouth with words from His heart to the one he leads me to share with today.

_____

_____

_____

_____

_____

_____

_____

_____

_____

_____

_____

_____

_____

_____

# DAY 81: ALL I NEED IS ALL OF YOU

"Beloved friends, what should be our proper response to God's marvelous mercies? I encourage you to surrender yourselves to God to be his sacred, living sacrifices. And live in holiness, experiencing all that delights his heart. For this becomes your genuine expression of worship. Stop imitating the ideals and opinions of the culture around you, but be inwardly transformed by the Holy Spirit through a total reformation of how you think. This will empower you to discern God's will as you live a beautiful life, satisfying and perfect in his eyes." Romans 12:1-2 TPT

**James 4:8, James 1:22, 1 John 2:3-6 TPT, 2 Timothy 2:20-21, 1 Corinthians 2:9, 2 Corinthians 3:18, 2 Corinthians 1:19-20, Ephesians 6:11-13, 2 Corinthians 4:18**

Beloved, I am near—I love to be near you. I am so pleased at the way you've absorbed My Word today. But don't just be a hearer of the Word: do what it says. This is how you begin to walk like Jesus did—in righteousness, truth, holiness, compassion, and in love. In love, I gave My life for you, dear one. In the same way, give yourself to others in love, to serve them. Preach the gospel and pray for the sick. You are my vessel... My hands and feet. Those who give Me their whole life will be amazed. No eye has seen, nor ear heard, the things which God has prepared for those who love me with agape love. I am good and My mercy endures forever. I am, daily, transforming you into My likeness. This is why you are noticing a larger gap between your desires and the desires of others around you. The things of this world will grow strangely dim, in the light of My glory and My grace. I am renewing your mind and heart to My truth and the purity of My Word.

I have heard your prayers and your requests. Declare My Word over your loved one that's running from Me. Do not bow to or agree with the enemy's schemes. Stand firm on My promises and decree them. Do not fear man, but only the Lord, your God. This is what separates My faithful, continually obedient ones from those who talk about Me, but do not walk in obedience. What others think or say is of no consequence to you, beloved. For it is written: *"Worship the Lord your God and serve him only." (Luke 4:8).* I am gazing at you, My child. I will strengthen you when you are weak. I will be your rest, your wisdom, and your unconditional love for others. This is easy for Me because unconditional love is who I am. I am aligning your heart with Mine. All I need is ALL OF YOU. Do not hold onto what the world has to give. It is temporary and will perish quickly. My treasures are eternal. In fact, you are one of My treasured ones. I will always be with you and forever you will be with Me.

## Declarations and Decrees of Truth

I decree and declare that I walk in the power of the Holy Spirit as I go today.

_____

_____

_____

_____

_____

_____

_____

_____

_____

_____

_____

_____

# Day 82: Foundational Keys
## of Identity

"Then God said, 'Let Us make man in Our image, according to Our likeness; let them have dominion over the fish of the sea, over the birds of the air, and over the cattle, over all the earth and over every creeping thing that creeps on the earth.' So God created man in His *own* image; in the image of God He created him; male and female He created them." Genesis 1:26-27 NKJV

**1 Corinthians 15:21-22, Romans 5:17-21, 1 Peter 4:8, Esther 5:1-3, Ephesians 1:22-23, Ephesians 2:6, John 14:13, Matthew 11:28, Job 22:28**

Beloved one, rejoice. You never go alone. Surrender your mouth to Me. I will pour out of it wisdom, truth, and love from your innermost being. I am faithful. Understanding foundational keys of identity found in My Word are very important. Go back to the garden with me, where things deviated from the original plan. Adam and Eve were made in My image. They were created for intimacy with their Father. They were created to reign and have dominion over the earth. What the first Adam lost that day, I came to regain... victory and dominion over sin and death. Because I am victorious, you are victorious. My love covered a multitude of sins. Put your confidence in Me. I always equip those I call... and I have called you. I want to clear this truth up in your own mind and thinking because you don't fully realize WHO YOU ARE. You are Mine, and I am above every name and authority in the universe. You are my bride—and like Esther had access to the Persian king in Babylon because she was his bride, so you have intimate access to Me, in My throne room. Ask me anything that aligns with My Word, in My name, and I will do it. You are seated with Me, to rule and reign on earth right now. You, when you know who you are, have royal identity. Begin to exercise this authority I have given you. I gave everything to get you back. I gave My very life for you. There's no greater love, My beloved. Lean into Me right now. I will go with you in every moment of your day. Release your burdens to Me. I am the God of the impossible. Everything will get done as I help you. Speak and decree who you are and what I've declared over you this day. My words bring life in every circumstance.

## Declarations and Decrees of Truth

I decree and declare that I am seated with Christ in heavenly places and as co-heir with Him, I have direct access to my Abba Father in heaven.

I decree and declare that I am bold and courageous because God is always with me.

_____

_____

_____

_____

_____

_____

_____

_____

_____

_____

_____

_____

_____

# DAY 83: TAKE HOLD OF WHO YOU ARE

"God always makes his grace visible in Christ, who includes us as partners of his endless triumph. Through our yielded lives he spreads the fragrance of the knowledge of God everywhere we go. We have become the unmistakable aroma *of the victory* of the Anointed One to God—a perfume of life to those being saved and the odor of death to those who are perishing. The unbelievers smell a deadly stench that leads to death, but believers smell the life-giving aroma that leads to abundant life. And who of us can rise to this challenge?" 2 Corinthians 2:14-16 TPT

**Psalm 81:10, Galatians 5:1, Ephesians 3:9-12, Matthew 11:12, John 20:22, Hebrews 11:6, Psalm 18:2, Psalm 42:16, 2 Corinthians 5:18-21, Isaiah 26:3, Romans 10:17, Isaiah 52:7, Isaiah 55:11**

My love for you rages like a fire, my child. I see your willing heart to go deeper with me. It pleases me when you prophesy. It shows your trust in Me. I am faithful to fill your mouth when you step into risk. I love to pour out My Spirit among My beloved children. Beautiful surrender and trust will begin to be established in My children's hearts. My will is freedom from all bondage, in order that each one of My sons and daughters may be filled with boldness to become love everywhere they go. Follow Me into the waters. I will hold your hand. Fix your eyes on Me and walk in purity. Do not forsake prayer. In that place, you will be filled each day with all My fullness. My kingdom is advancing, and I've called you to forcefully take hold of WHO YOU ARE and move in rhythm with Me. I'll never lead you where I don't go. Just as I breathe life into you, I want to use you to bring others to Me to also receive my breath of life. I am a rewarder of those who diligently seek Me. I am your rock, your fortress, your protector.

I am calling you to bring heaven to earth by walking on an unfamiliar path. But it's one of beauty, love, reconciliation, and hope. There are so many lost, hurting, and broken people, and so many are captive to the enemy's lies. You are My ambassador. You are My bride. I have given you the keys to My victory. Be steadfast in seeking Me daily. I am the bread of life. The manna of old was only good for one day. You need fresh manna from Me, daily, to sustain you. Reading My Word is foundational… and faith comes by hearing and hearing by the Word of God. I will draw near to you in every moment that you turn your thoughts toward Me. I AM has come near to you. I am equipping you in love, to be a world changer. So, take My light and My presence and My truth everywhere your feet tread. Stand firm on the foundation you've been given. As you open your mouth for My sake, I will fill it. My word does not return void, and my love never fails.

## Declarations and Decrees of Truth

I decree and declare I am not only a child of God, but I am a king and priest to the Lord.

# DAY 84: SET YOUR FEET UPON THE ROCK

"He lifted me out of the slimy pit, out of the mud and mire;
he set my feet on a rock and gave me a firm place to stand."
Psalm 40:2 NIV

**Psalm 55:22 ESV, Luke 10:38-42, Matthew 6:25-34, Job 22:28,
Romans 4:17, Matthew 28:19-20, Exodus 34:29, 2 John 1:6 NIV,
Matthew 10:37, Luke 12:48, Lamentations 3:22-23, Isaiah 26:3-4**

Beloved, words are really not adequate to describe My love. It is meant to be experienced. I love to demonstrate it to you for better understanding. My child, lay your burdens down right here at My feet. You act as though I've called you to a purpose but expect you to prepare for it without My help. Stop working like Martha and come to Me like Mary did. Trust Me. Be realistic. What are the things you need to do that are the highest priority? Do those things. Spend ample time with Me every day. Have I ever let you down? In your worry, you are communicating to Me a lack of trust. I am with you. Each morning, we will tackle the day together. Do not listen to the enemy's burden tactics. I am with you as I was with Moses and Joshua, Esther, Debra, Elisha, Daniel, Peter, Stephen, Paul and Silas, and John. In your faithfulness in coming to Me daily for relationship, you show Me you are fully committed to My kingdom and to loving My people. I will pick you up from the dust of despair and breathe courage and life into you. Set your feet upon the ROCK.

You have My authority and power to call things into existence that currently are not in existence. I am teaching you who you are. You are Mine and I have called you to go and make disciples. These disciples will, in turn, convert more disciples. My glory is upon you and My presence radiates from your skin. My Spirit loves to live in you. Obedience opens greater realms to My kingdom. Your faithfulness in the small is granting further access to greater anointings and callings. When much is given, much is required. I am heightening your detection of sin. I am calling you up into higher realms with Me. Devour My Word. As you study, go deep into the meaning as I lead you. There is much hidden treasure in My Holy Word.

Become the word. Do what it says. Submerse yourself in My truth. My voice will become louder in your soul. I've been watching as you turn your affection toward Me. I wait and wait to see if I am your greatest desire. I love to reward those who earnestly and diligently seek Me. Not for power, not for gifts—for an intimate relationship. My Father and I are gazing at you in this moment. I am the way, the truth, and the life. My pathway is life everlasting, for all who dare to follow me. I am your Shepherd and My compassion fails not. Great is my faithfulness.

### Declarations and Decrees of Truth:

I decree and declare that the Lord's peace is over my home, and joy is in every room.

_____

_____

_____

_____

_____

_____

_____

_____

_____

_____

_____

# Day 85: I Am Lighting the Way Before You

"This is the message we have heard from Him and announce to you, that God is Light, and in Him there is no darkness at all. If we say that we have fellowship with Him and yet walk in the darkness, we lie and do not practice the truth; but if we walk in the Light as He Himself is in the Light, we have fellowship with one another, and the blood of Jesus His Son cleanses us from all sin." 1 John 1:5-7 NASB

**Psalm 119:105, Ephesians 3:16-18, Isaiah 43:1-4,18-19, John 14:6, John 14:26, Psalm 139:12, Psalm 23, 2 Corinthians 5:18-21, John 15:4-7, Proverbs 22:6**

My Word is a lamp to your feet and a light to your path. I am near to you. My presence radiates from you, My child. My presence makes hearts tremble. It trembles yours, too. You are rooted and grounded in My love, and I am your strength. The enemy loves to speak and potter you through people in your life, but fear not, I have redeemed you, I have called you by name—you are Mine. I am lighting the way before you. I hold your hand on unfamiliar paths. Unfamiliar means something new and different. You are in a season of change. Cling to Me, beloved. I am the way, the truth, and the life. The enemy will lie to you about many things through many people, but the truth is found in Me. I have given you the Comforter because in this place of surrender, it can be uncomfortable. But the darkness isn't dark to Me. I will lead you in paths of righteousness because I am the Good Shepherd. I will search after My lost sheep. You are My courageous ambassador. Be an inspiration to those around you. Abide in Me and My Word. I AM the Word. Teach it to your kids. Be a voice in their life that is louder than the enemy's voice. And teach them to hear Mine. Who is more important to you than your very own offspring? Don't be idle but instruct them in love.

## Declarations and Decrees of Truth

I decree and declare that I clothe myself with compassion, kindness, humility, and gentleness.

I decree and declare that I do not pay back evil for evil, but I am patient and do good to everyone.

I decree and declare that no weapon formed against my family will prosper, in Jesus' name.

_____

_____

_____

_____

_____

_____

_____

_____

_____

_____

_____

_____

_____

_____

_____

_____

# DAY 86: IN ME... YOU ARE COMPLETE

"And our own completeness is now found in him. We are completely filled with God as Christ's fullness overflows within us. He is the Head of every kingdom and authority in the universe!" Colossians 2:10 TPT

**Hebrews 11:6, Matthew 24:14, Ephesians 5:1-2, Matthew 5:43, 1 John 4:4, Genesis 3, Isaiah 14:12-20, John 15:4, John 14:6, Deuteronomy 28:13**

Beloved, you are so loved by me. I reward your diligence. I see your affection every time you turn toward Me. I beckon you to come deeper with Me. My will for you is to become My Word. Read more. Speak to others from a place of experience. People need to hear the truth and the testimony of this simple gospel. Who will tell them if my church doesn't? No one desires hypocrisy. People want real love. Walk out My love today. Anyone can love their friends, but you must also love your enemies. This is how the world will see My love—through you. Trust Me, beloved. I don't send you into a den of lions, but if they come, I will shut their mouths. I am leading on you on a path that is unfamiliar because you have not walked here before. But I know the way, and I am greater than the one who is in the world.

In the garden, when sin came in, things were altered from Our original design. Therefore, the enemy became the ruler of the earth, and men's hearts were darkened. But I shined My light through My people, Israel. I kept my bloodline pure so my seed—Jesus, would be born of a woman and crush the enemy's head forever. At the right time, He will bring everything together under the authority of Himself—everything in heaven and on earth. I love My people on earth so much, I gave part of Myself, Jesus, to be a sacrifice, so you could live. We crushed sin and death—and made it so everyone who calls on the name of the Lord would be victorious. I came to crush death. So all the death, loss, and destruction going on began in the garden. This was not brought on by Me, nor sustained by Me. It was a deviation, and is what the devil thrives on, because he hates that you are sons of the Most High. He is rejected. Do not worry about the what-ifs. I am with you and I am holding you. You rest in Me and be faithful to do what I've called you to: stay connected to the vine. I am your Source. I am the way. I am the truth. I have given you life abundantly. You are Mine. Rejoice in Me and let your joy overflow... because in Me, you are complete.

## Declarations and Decrees of Truth

I decree and declare that I am complete in Christ and I cover all offenses with love.

---

---

---

---

---

---

---

---

---

---

---

---

---

---

# DAY 87: BELIEVE WHO YOU ARE AND BE FREE

"The mature children of God are those who are moved by the impulses of the Holy Spirit. And you did not receive the "spirit of religious duty," leading you back into the fear *of never being good enough*. But you have received the "Spirit of full acceptance," enfolding you into the family of God. And you will never feel orphaned, for as he rises up within us, our spirits join him in saying the words of tender affection, "Beloved Father!" For the Holy Spirit makes God's fatherhood real to us as he whispers into our innermost being, "You are God's beloved child!" Romans 8:14-16 TPT

**Zephaniah 3:17, 1 Samuel 16:7, 2 Corinthians 2:14-16, 2 Corinthians 3:17, 1 Corinthians 4:20, 2 Corinthians 6:17, Ephesians 4:23, 1 Corinthians 6:19, 2 Timothy 2:25-26, Isaiah 66:2**

Dear one, My heart was singing over you this morning. Man looks at the outward appearance, but I see the heart. I see yours. I drench you in My love in this moment. You are highly favored as my child. Walk in step with Me today. There are many on our path in need of My love. My presence is upon you... so release My presence over each person you show love to. My love reaches into dimly-lit places, as well as total darkness. I want to use you today to dispense the fragrance of heaven. It is a pleasing aroma to some, and a stench to others, but that is only the enemy's filter of lies. My love breaks through all the lies, and where My Spirit goes, there is freedom. Freedom for those that don't even know they are captive. My love prevails and it never fails.

Are you willing to live for Me whether you are working or playing? Many put Me on a shelf and declare their playtime as *their time*. But, loving people and spreading My fragrance is a part of who you are. Testify to My goodness and love everywhere you go, not just when you deem it necessary. My kingdom is one of power, not just words. Let truth sink deep into your heart, for it will transform you from the inside out. Then, you will be able to come out from among the world and it's tempting pleasures. My truth must transform your mind by renewing all the false thinking. My Spirit will not stop cleaning your temple as long as you remain humble before Me. As you draw closer to Me, I will draw closer to you. In this place, My Spirit and presence bring freedom. Freedom from the bondage that's kept you captive all these years. Captivity to the lies of the enemy—particularly about WHO YOU ARE, keeps many of My children in shackles. I desire their freedom from these lies. My Word, a humble heart, along with My Spirit, brings forth liberty.

## Declarations and Decrees of Truth

I decree and declare that I am a child of the Most High God, and I align my thoughts with the truth of the WORD of God.

# DAY 88: MY UNFAILING LOVE AND GRACE POUR OVER YOU

"And this hope will not lead to disappointment. For we know how dearly God loves us, because he has given us the Holy Spirit to fill our hearts with his love." Romans 5:5 ESV

**Revelation 22:13,16, Hebrews 1:3, John 10:27, Jeremiah 29:13, Hebrews 11:6, Isaiah 55:11, Isaiah 42:16, Romans 4:17, Revelation 1:8, Revelation 22:1-2**

Beloved, I am the bright morning star; I am the first and the last. I am the risen One. My heart delights in healing My people. In human form, I was the exact representation of the Father. When trouble befalls your children, did you allow it, or did it happen as a result of a fallen world? Do you help them? Rescue and restore them? Of course you do. So it is with our Father in heaven. He is the God who saves. Every child of God can hear their Father, but many aren't surrendered to put Me above all else. When they seek Me with all their heart, they will find Me. I reward those who diligently seek Me. I love to tenderly speak to those who are totally committed to Me and My kingdom. And My word does not return void. I cry out to you in your wilderness, and on an unfamiliar path I lead you. But, as you trust Me, beloved, we will go deeper. As you step out in greater measure, you will see many supernatural happenings. As you call into being the things which you do not see with your eyes, in faith, you will see creative miracles appear and it will astound many. Then they will know that I am the Lord... who was and is and is to come. My unfailing love and grace pour over those who lay down their lives for Me. All whose hearts who are totally committed to Me will see astounding works they have not conceived of ever before. My hand is with those who love Me completely and those who are sold out to My ways.

I am mighty to save and come near to the crushed in spirit. I exalt those who humble themselves before My mighty hand. Those who walk with Me will not stumble. I am the Lord your God who takes away the sins of the world. My love has been proven. I poured myself out for My people in unimaginable ways. Now you've been made righteous before Me, My child.

You have full access to My throne. Approach me. I am tender toward you, My child. My love drenches you like a waterfall and I never change. Come, drink from My river. It flows from My throne and it's not like anything you've ever experienced. All that I have is yours and I will never let you go.

## Declarations and Decrees of Truth

I decree and declare that I am EMPOWERED to flow in the gifts of the Holy Spirit.

I decree and declare that I will pray for others and see creative miracles that will astound many and draw people into God's love.

_____

_____

_____

_____

_____

_____

_____

_____

_____

_____

_____

_____

# DAY 89: I WILL HEAL THEM

"I, the Lord, have called you in righteousness; I will take hold of your hand. I will keep you and will make you to be a covenant for the people and a light for the Gentiles, to open eyes that are blind, to free captives from prison and to release from the dungeon those who sit in darkness...I will lead the blind by ways they have not known, along unfamiliar paths I will guide them; I will turn the darkness into light before them and make the rough places smooth. These are the things I will do; I will not forsake them." Isaiah 42:6-7,16 NIV

**Matthew 14:31, Job 33:4, Acts 17:24-28, 2 Corinthians 2:14-16, 1 Corinthians 2:10-16, John 14:26, Matthew 15:3-9, Isaiah 54:14, Psalm 103:1-14, Psalm 86:15, Psalm 145:8-9, Psalm 91:14-16, John 8:32**

Beloved one of Mine, you are hearing Me. How can you doubt? You have seen My words come to pass many times. I love to breathe life into you by communing with you. I enjoy drawing near to you. I am closer than your very breath. My presence radiates from your being. For some people you encounter, it will be a sweet aroma, and to others the smell of death. But it is My spirit in you that violates their conscience. Do not fear talking to these people. I wish to show them My love through you and to dispel the lies about who I am. I will speak through you and bring to mind My Word pertaining to this logic. "The way that seems right to men" is not My way. Many believe lies about Me because they believe the traditions they have always known, instead of being led into truth by My Spirit. My Spirit will show you the way as you abide in Me. Those who are afraid of My very Word are being deceived by the liar. They do not trust Me. They believe I give sickness. If they would surrender to Me, I would speak into their lives. But instead, they hold Me at arms-length because they don't know Me as *Father*. They beg me for healing because they think they are more compassionate than I am. But My mercy overflows.

I am leading the blind by ways they've not known. I will use your kind and gentle words to break down walls and point them to My loving ways. I will open the eyes of the blind and release the prisoners from the dungeons… I will rescue My people from the LIES. I am faithful to rescue those whom I love. Even in their stubborn pride, I show mercy. I will pursue them, and I will heal them.

## Declarations and Decrees of Truth

I decree and declare that I will not be deceived but live by the truth of the Word of God.
I decree and declare that I will speak life over every family member until I see breakthrough.

# DAY 90: CLING TO MY HAND, HERE WE GO!

"I drew you to myself from the ends of the earth and
called you from its farthest corner. I say to you: 'You are
my servant; I have chosen you. I have not rejected you!
Do not yield to fear, for I am always near. Never turn
your gaze from me, for I am your faithful God. I will
infuse you with my strength and help you in every situation. I will hold you firmly with my victorious right
hand.'" Isaiah 41:9-10 TPT

**Psalm 139:17-18, Hosea 6:6, 2 Chronicles 16:9,
Ephesians 5:2 TPT, 1 Corinthians 2:10 NLT**

My beloved one, yes, My thoughts toward you are many. I
love to lead you in paths of righteousness. My Word is a lamp
to your feet and a light to your path. But also, our intimate
communion is how I lead you down unfamiliar paths, holding
onto you every step of the way — even when you can't see your
next step. I am building in you… trust. Trust in Me, the Living
One. I hold your future in My hands and My plans are good. I
love to use you in My purposes, My child. My will is to draw
people unto Me and to love, heal, free, and rescue their eternal
spirits. So many are being deceived by the enemy of their soul.
Especially My well-meaning believers. They have a religion,
but I am not in religion. I am a relational Father. I desire mercy
over sacrifice. I want people's hearts. I'm not interested in
their personal striving. I gave everything for their salvation. I
am always looking to and fro, throughout the whole earth for
those hearts fully committed to Me. It is here that they find
the unwavering love and fullness of joy in Christ. Complete
abandonment to self… and total surrender… this is the place
in every heart that the kingdom of God will be made manifest.
Heaven meets earth. In this place, I can move supernaturally
and transform all who come to Me in desperation to know Me.
The One True God.

Oh, beloved, you are so pleasing to Me. I will continue to
bring heaven to earth through you when you step out in radical obedience to walk in love alongside those who are lost.

You have only scratched the surface of things you will see and experience as a vital part of My world colliding with yours. Hold onto Me. This adventure will be more than you could've dreamed, asked for, or imagined. I can't wait to adventure with you, My beautiful child. Focus your gaze intently on Me and listen as I tell you secrets about your life. Expect great things ahead of you. I am the Lord who parted the Red Sea for My people. There is nothing too grand or difficult for Me. I am with you mightily… rejoice. Your reward is found deeper. Deeper in me. Cling to My hand My child, here we go!

## Declarations and Decrees of Truth

I decree and declare that in every situation, God's hand holds me firmly, in Jesus' name.

_____

_____

_____

_____

_____

_____

_____

_____

_____

_____

_____

_____

# Appendix A

## Identity in Christ

### Child of God

*And because we are his children, God has sent the Spirit of his Son into our hearts, prompting us to call out, "Abba, Father." Now you are no longer a slave but God's own child. And since you are his child, God has made you his heir.*
*Galatians 4:6-7 NLT*

*And you did not receive the "spirit of religious duty," leading you back into the fear of never being good enough. But you have received the "Spirit of full acceptance", enfolding you into the family of God. And you will never feel orphaned, for as he rises up within us, our spirits join him in saying the words of tender affection, "Beloved Father!" For the Holy Spirit makes God's fatherhood real to us as he whispers into our innermost being, "You are God's beloved child!"*
*Romans 8:15-16 TPT*

### New Creation

*Therefore, if anyone is in Christ, he is a new creation. The old has passed away; behold, the new has come.*
*2 Corinthians 5:17 ESV*

*We were buried therefore with Him by the baptism into death, so that just as Christ was raised from the dead by the glorious [power] of the Father, so we too might [habitually] live and behave in newness of life. For if we have become one with Him by sharing a death like His, we shall also be [one with Him in sharing] His resurrection [by a new life lived for God].*                    Romans 6:4-5 AMPC

# Chosen

*Even as [in His love] He chose us [actually picked us out for Himself as His own] in Christ before the foundation of the world, that we should be holy (consecrated and set apart for Him) and blameless in His sight, even above reproach, before Him in love. For He foreordained us (destined us, planned in love for us) to be adopted (revealed) as His own children through Jesus Christ, in accordance with the purpose of His will [because it pleased Him and was His kind intent].*                    Ephesians 1:4-5 AMPC

# Masterpiece

*For we are God's masterpiece. He has created us anew in Christ Jesus, so we can do the good things he planned for us long ago.*                    Ephesians 2:10 NLT

# Forgiven

*But if we confess our sins to him, he is faithful and just to forgive us our sins and to cleanse us from all wickedness.*                    1 John 1:9 NLT

*And so, dear brothers and sisters, we can boldly enter heaven's Most Holy Place because of the blood of Jesus. By his death, Jesus opened a new and life-giving way through the curtain into the Most Holy Place. And since we have a great High Priest who rules over God's house, let us go right into the presence of God with sincere hearts fully trusting him. For our guilty consciences have been sprinkled with Christ's blood to make us clean, and our bodies have been washed with pure water.*                    Hebrews 10:17 NLT

## Sin is Crushed (Now we set our eyes on being sons, not sinners)

*We know that our old sinful selves were crucified with Christ so that sin might lose its power in our lives. We are no longer slaves to sin.*　　　　　　　　*Romans 6:6 NLT*

## Eternally and Unconditionally Loved

*The Lord appeared to us in the past, saying: "I have loved you with an everlasting love; I have drawn you with unfailing kindness."*　　　　　　*Jeremiah 31:3 NIV*

## Righteous, Holy, and Pure

*For God made the only one who did not know sin to become sin for us, so that we who did not know righteousness might become the righteousness of God through our union with him.*　　　　　　　　*2 Corinthians 5:21 TPT*

*He himself bore our sins in his body on the tree, that we might die to sin and live to righteousness. By his wounds you have been healed.*　　　　　　*1 Peter 2:24 ESV*

*Our faith in Jesus transfers God's righteousness to us and he now declares us flawless in his eyes. This means we can now enjoy true and lasting peace with God, all because of what our Lord Jesus, the Anointed One, has done for us... And there is still much more to say of his unfailing love for us! For through the blood of Jesus we have heard the powerful declaration, "You are now righteous in my sight." And because of the sacrifice of Jesus, you will never experience the wrath of God.*　　　　*Romans 5:1, 9 TPT*

## Secure in His Hand

*I give to them the gift of eternal life and they will never be lost, and no one has the power to snatch them out of my hands. My Father, who has given them to me as his gift, is the mightiest of all, and no one has the power to snatch them from my Father's care. The Father and I are one.*

*John 10:28-30 TPT*

*Those who live in the shelter of the Most High will find rest in the shadow of the Almighty. This I declare about the Lord: He alone is my refuge, my place of safety; he is my God, and I trust him. For he will rescue you from every trap and protect you from deadly disease. He will cover you with his feathers. He will shelter you with his wings. His faithful promises are your armor and protection. Do not be afraid of the terrors of the night, nor the arrow that flies in the day. Do not dread the disease that stalks in darkness, nor the disaster that strikes at midday. Though a thousand fall at your side, though ten thousand are dying around you, these evils will not touch you. Just open your eyes and see how the wicked are punished. If you make the Lord your refuge, if you make the Most High your shelter, no evil will conquer you; no plague will come near your home. For he will order his angels to protect you wherever you go. They will hold you up with their hands, so you won't even hurt your foot on a stone. You will trample upon lions and cobras; you will crush fierce lions and serpents under your feet! The Lord says, "I will rescue those who love me. I will protect those who trust in my name. When they call on me, I will answer; I will be with them in trouble. I will rescue and honor them. I will reward them with a long life and give them my salvation."*
*Psalms 91:1-16 NLT*

## Alive to the Spirit, Dead to the Flesh

*Since you have heard about Jesus and have learned the truth that comes from him, throw off your old sinful nature and your former way of life, which is corrupted by lust and deception. Instead, let the Spirit renew your thoughts and attitudes. Put on your new nature, created to be like God — truly righteous and holy.*
*Ephesians 4:21-24 NLT*

*As you yield freely and fully to the dynamic life and power of the Holy Spirit, you will abandon the cravings of your self-life. For your self-life craves the things that offend the Holy Spirit and hinder him from living free within you! And the Holy Spirit's intense cravings hinder your old self-life from dominating you! So then, the two incompatible and conflicting forces within you are your self-life of the flesh and the new creation life of the Spirit. But when you are brought into the full freedom of the Spirit of grace, you will no longer be living under the domination of the law but soaring above it!*        *Galatians 5:16-18 TPT*

## Salt, Light, and LOVE

*You are the salt of the earth, but if salt has lost its taste, how shall its saltiness be restored? It is no longer good for anything except to be thrown out and trampled under people's feet. "You are the light of the world. A city set on a hill cannot be hidden. Nor do people light a lamp and put it under a basket, but on a stand, and it gives light to all in the house. In the same way, let your light shine before others, so that they may see your good works and give glory to your Father who is in heaven.*    *Matthew 5:13-16 ESV*

*Now, because of your obedience to the truth, you have purified your very souls, and this empowers you to be full of love for your fellow believers. So express this sincere love toward one another passionately and with a pure heart.*
*1 Peter 1:22 TPT*

## Bride of Christ

*(Paul speaking to the church in Corinth) You need to know that God's passion is burning inside me for you, because, like a loving father, I have pledged your hand in marriage to Christ, your true bridegroom. I've also promised that I would present his fiancée to him as a pure virgin bride.*
*2 Corinthians 11:2 TPT*

*Let us rejoice and exalt him and give him glory, because the wedding celebration of the Lamb has come. And his bride has made herself ready. Fine linen, shining bright and clear, has been given to her to wear, and the fine linen represents the righteous deeds of his holy believers.*

*Revelation 19:7-8 TPT*

## Full Surrender to Jesus

*I have been crucified with Christ and I no longer live, but Christ lives in me. The life I now live in the body, I live by faith in the Son of God, who loved me and gave himself for me.*

*Galatians 2:20 NIV*

## Ambassador for Jesus (His Representative)

*And God has made all things new, and reconciled us to himself, and given us the ministry of reconciling others to God. In other words, it was through the Anointed One that God was shepherding the world, not even keeping records of their transgressions, and he has entrusted to us the ministry of opening the door of reconciliation to God. We are ambassadors of the Anointed One who carry the message of Christ to the world, as though God were tenderly pleading with them directly through our lips. So we tenderly plead with you on Christ's behalf, "Turn back to God and be reconciled to him."*

*2 Corinthians 5:18-20 TPT*

## Victorious

*But thanks be to God! He gives us the victory through our Lord Jesus Christ.*

*1 Corinthians 15:57 NIV*

*Yet even in the midst of all these things, we triumph over them all, for God has made us to be more than conquerors, and his demonstrated love is our glorious victory over everything!*

*Romans 8:37 TPT*

# Inheritance in Christ

*Your hearts can soar with joyful gratitude when you think of how God made you worthy to receive the glorious inheritance freely given to us by living in the light. He has rescued us completely from the tyrannical rule of darkness and has translated us into the kingdom realm of his beloved Son.*
*Colossians 1:12-13 TPT*

*Now we have been stamped with the seal of the promised Holy Spirit. He is given to us like an engagement ring is given to a bride, as the first installment of what's coming! He is our hope-promise of a future inheritance which seals us until we have all of redemption's promises and experience complete freedom — all for the supreme glory and honor of God!*
*Ephesians 1:13b-14 TPT*

# Called to Abide and Have Full Communion

*So you must remain in life-union with me, for I remain in life-union with you. For as a branch severed from the vine will not bear fruit, so your life will be fruitless unless you live your life intimately joined to mine.*
*John 15:4 TPT*

*Those who are loved by God, let his love continually pour from you to one another, because God is love. Everyone who loves is fathered by God and experiences an intimate knowledge of him.*
*1 John 4:7 TPT*

# Carrier of the Holy Spirit Without Limit

*For indeed, we are the temple of the living God, just as God has said: 'I will make my home in them and walk among them. I will be their God, and they will be my people.'*
*2 Corinthians 6:16b TPT*

*But the fruit produced by the Holy Spirit within you is divine love in all its varied expressions: joy that overflows, peace that subdues, patience that endures, kindness in action, a life full of virtue, faith that prevails, gentleness of heart, and strength of spirit. Never set the law above these qualities, for they are meant to be limitless.*

*Galatians 5:22-23 TPT*

*The One whom God has sent to represent him will speak the words of God, for God has poured out upon him the fullness of the Holy Spirit without limitation.*

*John 3:34 TPT*

*[Jesus prayed in the garden] Just as You commissioned and sent Me into the world, I also have commissioned and sent them (believers) into the world. For their sake I sanctify Myself [to do Your will], so that they also may be sanctified [set apart, dedicated, made holy] in [Your] truth. I do not pray for these alone [it is not for their sake only that I make this request], but also for [all] those who [will ever] believe and trust in Me through their message...*

*John 17:18-20 AMP*

## Partakers of the Divine Nature

*"His divine power has granted to us all things that pertain to life and godliness, through the knowledge of him who called us to his own glory and excellence, by which he has granted to us his precious and very great promises, so that through them you may become **partakers of the divine nature**, having escaped from the corruption that is in the world because of sinful desire."*     *2 Peter 1:3-4 ESV*

## Joint-heirs with Jesus Christ

*So you are no longer a slave, but God's child; and since you are his child, God has made you also an heir.*

*Galatians 4:7 NIV*

*And if children, then heirs; heirs of God, and joint-heirs with Christ; if so be that we suffer with him, that we may be also glorified together.*        Romans 8:17 NKJV

*And He raised us up together with Him and made us sit down together [giving us joint seating with Him] in the heavenly sphere [by virtue of our being] in Christ Jesus (the Messiah, the Anointed One). He did this that He might clearly demonstrate through the ages to come the immeasurable (limitless, surpassing) riches of His free grace (His unmerited favor) in [His] kindness and goodness of heart toward us in Christ Jesus.*        Ephesians 2:6-7 AMPC

# Appendix B

## NOW is the Time for Salvation

Giving your life to Jesus is the most important decision anyone can make in this life, because it determines your where you will spend eternity. This decision is about to change your eternal destination forever. You're becoming a part of a new family.

This is not something you have to redo and pray over and over. If you are genuine in your surrender, Jesus will take your life and transform it completely.

Salvation in Jesus Christ is not just repeating words or agreeing with a set of facts. It is an encounter with the Living Jesus.

Encountering Jesus makes you aware that you need forgiveness for your sin.

> *Jesus replied, "I tell you the truth, everyone who sins is a slave of sin.*　　　　　　　　　　　　　　*John 8:34 NLT*

It is astounding to realize the Bible says Jesus laid His life down for you right in the middle of your mess. That is how much He loves YOU.

> *But God demonstrates his own love for us in this: While we were still sinners, Christ died for us.*
> 　　　　　　　　　　　　　　　　　　*Romans 5:8 NIV*

Our sin deserved death, but our God is a WAYMAKER. He gave us His only son, Jesus, to make a way for us to be saved.

> *For the wages of sin is death, but the free gift of God is*
> *eternal life through Christ Jesus our Lord.*
> *Romans 6:23 NLT*

Just knowing information about salvation isn't enough. The Bible says even the demons know all these things. But they hate the truth.

Salvation is asking to begin a RELATIONSHIP with your Lord and Savior… and as you give your life to Him, you are truly trusting Him to save you and fully forgive you from all of your sin. This is not just a head knowledge, it's a heart connection also. A personal connection between you and Jesus… you don't become saved because people in your family have trusted him. Salvation is personal. It is for individuals.

> *John 3:16 says, "WHOEVER believes in him will not perish,*
> *but have eternal life." NIV*

He has been pursuing you. Waiting on you to come to Him. The next few words are not magic and the words themselves do not save you. But they will help you express your heart to HIM.

**Lord Jesus, I come to ask You to forgive me for my sins for the past, present, and future. I believe that You not only died for my sins but rose again and conquered death. I confess that I want You to be my Lord and Savior forever. I give my life to You, completely, to transform me into the one you created me to be. Today, I want a relationship with You. Holy Spirit, I invite You into my life, to fill me, and connect God's voice to my heart.**

**In Jesus' name, Amen.**

# Appendix C

## Book Recommendations

### God's presence:

Practicing His Presence
by Brother Lawrence and Frank Laubach

### Fasting:

Atomic Power with God, Thru Fasting and Prayer
by Franklin Hall

### Healing, Identity, and Prophesy:

Biblical Basis for Healing
By Randy Clark

Essential Guide to Healing
By Randy Clark and Bill Johnson

Do What Jesus Did
By Robby Dawkins

Identity Thief
By Robby Dawkins

When Everything Changes: Healing, Justice, and the Kingdom of God
By Steve Stewart

<u>Divine Healing Made Simple</u>
By Praying Medic

<u>Translating God</u>
By Shawn Bolz

## Video Recommendations:

<u>Finger of God 2</u>
WP Films (There are many other documentaries they have produced that are excellent.)
WPfilm.com, or subscribe at WPfilms.TV

## YouTube Recommended Channels:

I have learned so much about identity, healing, prophecy, power evangelism and spiritual warfare from trusted ministries on YouTube.

- Todd White
  Lifestylechristianity.com
- Robby Dawkins
  Robbydawkins.com
- Eric Gilmour
  Sonship-international.org
- Brian Guerin
  Bridalglory.com
- Dan Mohler
- Jesus Image
- Preacher Talks
- Randy Clark (Globalawakening.com)
- Graham Cooke
- Robert Morris (Gatewaychurch.tv)
- Bill Johnson

- Kris Vallotton
- Patricia King
- Sandra Kennedy

# End Notes

---

1. "Word", *KJV with Strong's Concordance:* Romans 10:17 (Bible Explore.com. http://www.godrules.net/library/kjvstrongs/kjvstrongs.htm), #G4487.

2. A.W. Tozer, *The Knowledge of the Holy* (New York: Harper Collins, 1978), 1.

3. Frank Laubach, and Brother Lawrence, *Practicing His Presence* (Jacksonville: The Seed Sowers, 1973), 85.

4. Lawrence, Brother. YouVersion app. Version 8.13.2. 2019. *Practicing the Presence of God: Exploring an Old Habit for a New Year,* Devotional for Download. YouVersion.com (accessed on 2/9/2019).

5. *Finger of God 2,* Dir. Will Hacker. Perf Daniel Kolenda(WP Films, 2018), christian documentary film.

6. "Disciple", **Cambridge Academic Content Dictionary** (© Cambridge University Press, 2019), dictionary.cambridge.org/disciple.

7. John Wimber and Kevin Springer, *Power Evangelism* (Minneapolis: Chosen Books, 2009), Kindle Books, Epub file, 24 Mar. 2019.

8. Randy Clark, *Biblical Basis for Healing:*(ePub. 2011), 43.

# Bibliography

Tozer, A.W. *The Knowledge of the Holy.* New York: Harper Collins, 1978, 1.

Clark, Randy. *Biblical Basis for Healing:* ePub. 2011, 43.

"Disciple." **Cambridge Academic Content Dictionary** © Cambridge University Press, 2019, dictionary.cambridge. org/disciple.

*Finger of God 2.* Dir. Will Hacker. Perf Daniel Kolenda. WP Films, 2018, Christian documentary film.

Laubach, Frank and Lawrence, Brother. *Practicing His Presence.* Jacksonville: The Seedsowers, 1973. Print. 85.

Lawrence, Brother. YouVersion app. Version 8.13.2. 2019. *Practicing the Presence of God: Exploring an Old Habit for a New Year,* Devotional for Download. YouVersion.com (accessed on 2/9/2019).

Wimber, John and Springer, Kevin. *Power Evangelism.* Minneapolis: Chosen Books, 2009. Kindle Books. Epub file. 24 Mar. 2019.

"Word." *KJV with Strong's Concordance.* #G4487. Romans 10:17, Bible Explore.com. http://www.godrules.net/library/kjvstrongs/kjvstrongs.htm

CPSIA information can be obtained
at www.ICGtesting.com
Printed in the USA
JSHW011441121219
2898JS00001B/1